An Introduction
to Fuzzy Logic
for Practical Applications

Springer
New York
Berlin
Heidelberg
Barcelona
Budapest
Hong Kong
London
Milan
Paris
Santa Clara
Singapore
Tokyo

An Introduction to Fuzzy Logic for Practical Applications

Kazuo Tanaka

Translated by Tak Niimura

With 82 Illustrations

 Springer

Kazuo Tanaka
Department of Mechanical Systems Engineering
Kanazawa University
2-40-20 Kodatsuro
Kanazawa 920
Japan

First published in Japanese by Rassel, Inc. in 1991.

Library of Congress Cataloging-in-Publication Data
Tanaka, Kazuo, 1962–
    An introduction to fuzzy logic for practical applications / by
Kazuo Tanaka: translated by Tak Niimura.
      p.   cm.
    Includes bibliographical references and index.
    ISBN 0-387-94807-4 (softcover : alk. paper)
    1. Fuzzy logic.   I. Title.
QA9.64.T36   1996
511.3—dc20   96-19133

Printed on acid-free paper.

Production managed by Robert Wexler; manufacturing supervised by Jeffrey Taub.
Typeset by The Bartlett Press, Marietta, GA.
Printed and bound by Braun-Brumfield, Inc., Ann Arbor, MI.
Printed in the United States of America.

9 8 7 6 5 4 3 2 1

ISBN 0-387-94807-4   Springer-Verlag New York Berlin Heidelberg   SPIN 10540167

Contents

1

Introduction

This chapter gives an outline and the historical background of fuzzy set theory and its applications. It also introduces the structure of this book.

1.1 What is Fuzzy Logic?

Fuzzy logic was born in 1965. In that year, Lotfi Zadeh of the University of California, Berkeley, published a paper titled "Fuzzy Sets" in the journal *Information and Control* [1]. This paper is said to have been completed more than two years before its publication but no technical journals dared to accept the paper because of its radical idea. It was inconceivable to allow vagueness in the engineering field at that time. Only *Information and Control* would accept his paper because he was the editor of the journal. Zadeh later proposed the idea of the fuzzy algorithm, which laid the foundation of fuzzy logic and reasoning. In 1972 Michio Sugeno of the Tokyo Institute of Technology followed Zadeh with the concepts of fuzzy measure and fuzzy integral.

A turning point for fuzzy logic came in 1974. Ebraham Mamdani of the University of London applied fuzzy logic to controls for the first time—the control of a simple steam engine [2]. The first industrial application appeared six years later. In 1980, F. H. Smidth of Denmark first applied fuzzy logic to the control of a cement kiln. In the 1980s, Fuji Electric of Japan applied fuzzy logic to the control of a water purification process and later Hitachi developed an automatic train control system with fuzzy logic. These were the forerunners of the fuzzy logic "boom" in Japan in the early 1990s.

The International Fuzzy System Association (IFSA) was established in 1984 as the first academic organization for fuzzy logic theorists and practitioners. IFSA holds an international symposium every other year. Around the same time, practical applications began to be reported in Japan particularly in the control field. In 1989, the Society of Fuzzy Theory and Systems (SOFT) was founded and the Laboratory of International Fuzzy Engineering (LIFE) was inaugurated in Japan. In the early 1990s, fuzzy logic was applied to home electronics products and the nonengineering public became aware of fuzzy systems.

When the first paper on fuzzy logic was published in 1965, a new control method using state space proposed by Rudolf Kalman [3] was beginning to be recognized as "modern control." Shortly before that time, Zadeh was researching related subjects such as z-transform, and he has done some pioneering work in the field. It is very interesting to note that he turned from precise control engineering to fuzzy logic, which allows vagueness. He later said that he saw the limitation of such preciseness. He referred to this idea as the "principle of incompatibility" in his 1973 paper [4]. The principle of incompatibility claims that as the complexity of a system exceeds a certain limit, precise and meaningful description of the system's behavior becomes impossible. I think the "principle of incompatibility" is the origin of fuzzy logic.

Fuzzy logic is a broad theory including fuzzy set theory, fuzzy logic, fuzzy measure, and others. Fuzzy set theory is an extension of conventional set theory. Fuzzy logic is an extension of conventional (binary) logic. Fuzzy measure is an extension of probability measure. Fuzziness, as handled in fuzzy logic, can refer to various types of vagueness and uncertainty but particularly to the vagueness related to human linguistics and thinking, and it is different from the uncertainty handled by probability theory. Probabilistic uncertainty is, for example, the chance of getting three by throwing a die. Probabilistic uncertainty can be judged objectively by repeated trials. For example, the chance of getting three by throwing a die can converge into one-sixth after trying infinite times.

On the other hand, the criteria for words such as "pretty" and "young" depend on the person who judges and we cannot construct a strict basis for them even by endless trial and experiments. For example, a girl next door may look "pretty" to me but not to her father. A 30-year-old man may be "young" on a cruise ship but not "young" in a discotheque. Such words as "pretty" and "young" are rather subjective and depend on situations. Fuzzy logic can handle such vagueness mathematically.

Let us look at the application aspect of fuzzy logic then. The earliest and most successful applications have been in the control field. By the time of this writing, various applications from large plants such as steel mills, glass processing, fermentation, water purification, and power utilities, to small appliances such as video cameras and washing machines have sprouted.

Also, application to knowledge processing has been aggressively promoted. Several decision support systems have been commercialized and other applications such as medical diagnostics, fault analysis, investment consultation, bus transit scheduling, and management strategy are rapidly increasing. All these applications aim at representing the human ability of knowledge processing on computers. In recent years, nonengineering applications such as social and environmental systems have been tested and they are expected to bear fruit.

We can expect that the number of application fields of fuzzy logic will continue to grow. There are many fields of application but we should always bear in mind how to apply fuzzy logic to make the application most effective. For that goal, we need to grasp the essence of fuzzy logic.

1.2 Structure of This Book

As stated earlier, fuzzy logic can be applied to various fields. The essential concepts of fuzzy logic for application are fuzzy sets, fuzzy relations, and fuzzy (approximate) reasoning. This book covers all these essentials. The last chapter of this book describes fuzzy logic control. Fuzzy logic control was the first application of fuzzy logic to practical systems and has proved to be very successful. Fuzzy logic control can also be assumed as an application of fuzzy reasoning. The description of fuzzy logic control focuses on the application of fuzzy reasoning and does not require background knowledge of control theory.

The contents of this book are: Chapter 2. Fuzzy Set Theory, Chapter 3. Fuzzy Relations, Chapter 4. Fuzzy Reasoning (Approximate Reasoning), and Chapter 5. Fuzzy Logic Control.

In this book two types of square frames appear to notify readers of essential ideas of fuzzy logic. They are used as follows.

═══ [double square] ═══ · · · Definitions;
─── [single square] ─── · · · Other important properties.

References

[1] Zadeh, L. A. 1965. Fuzzy sets. *Information and Control* 8; 338–353.
[2] Mamdani, E. H. 1974. Applications of fuzzy algorithms for control of a simple dynamic plant. *Proceedings IEE*, 121, 12; 1585–1588.
[3] Kalman, R. E. (1960) A new approach to linear filtering and prediction problems, *Transactions ASME Journal Basic Engineering series*. D82, 35–46.
[4] Zadeh, L. A. 1973. Outline of a new approach to the analysis of complex systems and decision process. *IEEE Transactions* SMC-3, 1; 28–44.

2

Fuzzy Set Theory

In this chapter, essentials of fuzzy set theory, aimed at applications, are introduced. The definition and fundamental properties of fuzzy sets are described and compared to conventional sets. Operation of fuzzy sets, α-cut, and the decomposition principle are also given. Then fuzzy numbers and extension principles are presented.

2.1 Fuzzy Sets

An everyday conversation contains many vague words from such gossip as "The girl next door is pretty," to an economist's statement that "The dollar is getting relatively strong." Fuzzy sets were proposed to deal with such vague words and expressions. Fuzzy sets can handle such vague concepts as "a set of *tall* people" and "the people living *close* to Tokyo," which are unable to be expressed by conventional set theory. In the preceding expressions, the words "tall" and "close" give ambiguous ideas. These vague expressions are not allowed in conventional set theory and we have to define terms exactly like "the set of people more than 190 cm in height," or "the people living in Tokyo." A measurement of a person's height will show if the person belongs to the former group. These conventional sets, which are defined exactly, are called "crisp sets" in fuzzy set theory.

I will describe crisp set theory before introducing fuzzy set theory. Fuzzy set theory is an extension of crisp set theory and the comprehension of fuzzy set theory will be difficult without knowing crisp set theory. However, because the goal of this book is the application of fuzzy logic, I limit the description of crisp sets to the basics.

2.1.1 Crisp Sets and Characteristic Functions

In crisp set theory, union, intersection, and complement are defined as follows.

Union, intersection, and complement of crisp sets

Let A, B represent subsets of the universe X. Union, intersection, and complement are defined as follows.

- Union of crisp sets A and B:

$$A \cup B = \{x \mid x \in A \text{ or } x \in B\}. \tag{2.1}$$

- Intersection of crisp sets A and B:

$$A \cap B = \{x \mid x \in A \text{ and } x \in B\}, \tag{2.2}$$

- Complement of crisp set A:

$$\overline{A} = \{x \mid x \notin A\}. \tag{2.3}$$

The preceding definitions of union, intersection, and complement are illustrated in Figure 2.1. Figures such as these are called Venn diagrams or Euler diagrams.

Let us represent that A, B are subsets of the universe X by $A \subset X$ and $B \subset X$. When we say "A is a subset of X," it means that any element of the set A belongs to X. For example, let

$$X = \{1, 2, 3, 4, 5, 6, 7, 8, 9, 10\}$$
$$A = \{2, 4, 6, 8, 10\}$$
$$B = \{-3, 0, 3\}.$$

Then $A \subset X$ but $B \not\subset X$. Here $B \not\subset X$ indicates that B is not a subset of X.

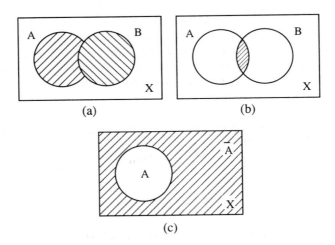

FIGURE 2.1. (a) Union, (b) intersection, and (c) complement of crisp sets.

For the preceding sets, we note the following properties:

- union: $A \subset (A \cup B), B \subset (A \cup B)$
- intersection: $(A \cap B) \subset A, (A \cap B) \subset B$
- complement: $A \cup \overline{A} = X$ (The law of excluded middle)

  $A \cap \overline{A} = \varnothing$ (The law of contradiction)

where $\varnothing$ means an empty set.

These properties can be verified by Venn diagrams. Other properties are summarized as follows.

Properties of crisp sets

- Idempotent law:

$$A \cup A = A, \qquad A \cap A = A. \tag{2.4}$$

- Commutative law:

$$A \cup B = B \cup A, \qquad A \cap B = B \cap A. \tag{2.5}$$

- Associative law:

$$A \cup (B \cup C) = (A \cup B) \cup C,$$
$$A \cap (B \cap C) = (A \cap B) \cap C. \tag{2.6}$$

- Distributive law:

$$A \cup (B \cap C) = (A \cup B) \cap (A \cup C),$$
$$A \cap (B \cup C) = (A \cap B) \cup (A \cap C). \tag{2.7}$$

- The law of double negation:

$$A = \overline{\overline{A}}. \tag{2.8}$$

- De Morgan's law:

$$\overline{A \cup B} = \overline{A} \cap \overline{B},$$
$$\overline{A \cap B} = \overline{A} \cup \overline{B}. \tag{2.9}$$

EXAMPLE 2.1. UNION, INTERSECTION, AND COMPLEMENT OF CRISP SETS

A tennis club to which Bob belongs includes six members. Let us think of sets of females and students. The universe in this case is the set of all members which is defined as:

members = {Anne, Bob, Cathy, John, Linda, Tom}.

Let us form a female set out of the preceding set.

female members = {Anne, Cathy, Linda}.

Also, the set of students will be:

  student members = {Bob, John, Linda}.

Here, if we assign the preceding sets as

  X :   members,
  A :   female members, and
  B :   student members,

the relationship of the sets can be illustrated by a Venn diagram as shown in Figure 2.2.

  Union, intersection, and complement of A and B are as follows.

  $A \cup B$ = {Anne, Bob, Cathy, John, Linda}
  $A \cap B$ = {Linda}
     $\overline{A}$ = {Bob, John, Tom}
     $\overline{B}$ = {Anne, Cathy, Tom}.

Here $A \cup B$ is the set of female or student members, $A \cap B$ is the set of female student members, $\overline{A}$ is the set of nonfemale (male) members, and $\overline{B}$ is the set of nonstudent members.

  We also observe that

  $\overline{A \cup B} = \overline{A} \cap \overline{B}$ = {Tom}
  $\overline{A \cap B} = \overline{A} \cup \overline{B}$ = {Anne, Bob, Cathy, John, Tom},

verifying De Morgan's law.

  It is no trouble to write down the elements of the sets if, as in this example, the number of elements is small. However, it can be a nuisance if there are many elements. For example, it is easy to write

  A = {1, 2, 3, 4, 5, 6, 7, 8, 9, 10}

but if

  A = {1, 2, 3, ..., 98, 99, 100},

it is more convenient to write

  $A = \{x \mid 1 \le x \le 100 \text{ and } x \text{ being integer}\}$.

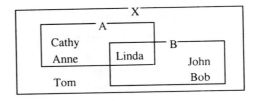

FIGURE 2.2. Venn diagram of tennis club members.

In general, crisp sets are defined by characteristic functions as follows.

Characteristic functions

Let A represent a crisp set on the universe X. Its characteristic function χ_A can be defined by a mapping

$$\chi_A : X \rightarrow \{0, 1\} \tag{2.10}$$

as

$$\chi_A(x) = \begin{cases} 1 & x \in X \\ 0 & x \notin X \end{cases} . \tag{2.11}$$

(2.11) indicates that if the element x belongs to A, χ_A is 1, and if it does not belong to A, χ_A is 0.

Characteristic functions are rarely used for the application of crisp sets. However, when we extend this idea to fuzzy sets, the role of characteristic functions becomes significant as shown in Section 2.1.2.

2.1.2 Fuzzy Sets and Membership Functions

Whereas crisp sets can be defined by characteristic functions, fuzzy sets can be characterized by membership functions. Before going into the definition of membership functions, let us review the case given in Example 2.1.

EXAMPLE 2.2. FUZZY SETS AND CRISP SETS

The sets used in the previous example are:

X: members,

A: female members, and

B: student members.

In this example, we replace the crisp sets A and B with the following fuzzy sets $\widetilde{A}$ and $\widetilde{B}$:

$\widetilde{A}$:   the set of overweight people;

$\widetilde{B}$:   the set of people of moderate height.

It is inconvenient to express these fuzzy sets by Venn diagram because the ideas of "overweight" and "moderate height" are different from person to person and dependent on the situation. It is impractical to divide people into a "overweight" group and a "not overweight" group. The degree of "overweight" can vary from "a little heavy" to "extremely heavy." Therefore it is necessary to express the degree of being "overweight." In this example, we try to assign a real number between 0 and 1 to a degree. The degree 1 means the person completely belongs to the set

TABLE 2.1.   Degrees of "overweight" and "moderate height."

Set	Anne	Bob	Cathy	John	Linda	Tom
overweight	0.5	0.9	0.3	0.4	0.7	0.6
moderate height	0.4	0.1	0.5	0.7	0.9	0.8

of "overweight people" and 0 denotes the person does not belong to the set. In this case, suppose that we can express the degrees of "overweight" and "moderate height" as in Table 2.1.

Membership functions of fuzzy sets define the degree shown in the table. In the characteristic function of crisp sets, we have to decide the degree, either 0 or 1, whereas membership functions allow us to choose an arbitrary real value between 0 and 1.

In the preceding example I have distinguished fuzzy sets such as $\tilde{A}$ and $\tilde{B}$ using $\sim$ signs. Hereafter, in this book, I do not use $\sim$ unless we have to distinguish fuzzy sets explicitly from crisp sets.

Fuzzy sets can be assumed to be an extension of crisp sets. Therefore, membership functions are the extension of characteristic functions.

Fuzzy sets and membership functions

A fuzzy (sub-) set A on the universe X is a set defined by a membership function μ_A representing a mapping

$$\mu_A : X \rightarrow \{0, 1\}. \tag{2.12}$$

Here the value of $\mu_A(x)$ for the fuzzy set A is called the membership value or the grade of membership of $x \in X$. The membership value represents the degree of x belonging to the fuzzy set A.

The value of the characteristic functions for crisp sets defined in (2.11) was either 0 or 1 but the membership value of a fuzzy set can be an arbitrary real value between 0 and 1 as indicated by (2.12). The closer the value of $\mu_A(x)$ to 1, the higher the grade of membership of the element x in fuzzy set A. If $\mu_A(x) = 1$, the element x completely belongs to the fuzzy set A. If $\mu_A(x) = 0$, the element x does not belong to A at all.

EXAMPLE 2.3. MEMBERSHIP FUNCTIONS AND CHARACTERISTIC FUNCTIONS

In this example I compare membership functions and characteristic functions to demonstrate the features of fuzzy sets. There are several examples of fuzzy sets based on a person's height. Figures 2.3 and 2.4 show the characteristic functions and membership functions, respectively, for "low," "middle," and "high" stature.

Suppose now the height of three persons A, B, C is given as:

A: 178 cm,

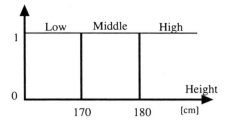

FIGURE 2.3. Crisp sets of height.

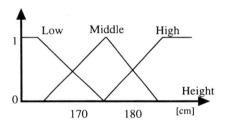

FIGURE 2.4. Fuzzy sets of height.

B: 166 cm,

C: 181 cm.

If we compare the individual height with the crisp set defined in Figure 2.3, we can obtain the value of the characteristic function as in Table 2.2.

The value of the characteristic function indicates A and B belong to the "Middle" height set, and C belongs to the Low set. However, A or C may feel unhappy about the division because the difference in height of B and C is only 3 cm, whereas the difference between A and B is 8 cm and they belong to the same group. This is due to the division of "Middle" height set between 170 cm and 180 cm. In crisp sets different results may follow a different division.

On the other hand, we get the membership value of individual height comparing the fuzzy sets shown in Figure 2.4 and the value of the actual height. Table 2.3

TABLE 2.2.   The value of characteristic functions in crisp sets.

	Height	Low	Middle	High
A	179 cm	0	1	0
B	171 cm	0	1	0
C	168 cm	1	0	0

TABLE 2.3.   Value of membership functions in fuzzy sets.

	Height	Low	Middle	High
A	179 cm	0	0.4	0.6
B	171 cm	0.4	0.6	0
C	168 cm	0.7	0.3	0

shows such membership value. This table shows, for example, A belongs to the "Middle" set in the grade of 0.4 and to the "High" set in the grade of 0.6, whereas A does not belong to the "Low" set. If we are to express their height linguistically, the expression may be as follows:

A: higher middle,

B: lower middle,

C: relatively low.

When we express height in fuzzy sets, the division will not result in a compelling difference as in the crisp set case, and each individual will likely be satisfied with the result. Fuzzy sets can thus give opportunities to express such sensible matter in a manner that is much closer to human feeling than crisp sets.

Fuzzy sets need to be defined properly to reflect the situation. For example, the meaning of "fast" and "middle" may be different depending on the situation. Let us discuss the "proper" definition of fuzzy sets in the following example.

EXAMPLE 2.4. DEFINITION OF FUZZY SETS DEPENDING ON SITUATIONS

When we think of the speed of a car, the interpretation of how "fast" the car is going is different whether it is running on an ordinary road or on a highway. Figure 2.5 shows the difference of the definition of fuzzy set "fast." The speed of 80 km/h may likely be considered "fast" on an ordinary road but it is not "fast" on a highway.

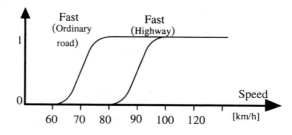

FIGURE 2.5. Difference in speed of car depending on situation.

Another example is the fuzzy sets that represents "moderate" height. The interpretation of "moderate" height is different, for example, from one country to another and it also varies from one sport to another. The average height of an American male is higher than that of a Japanese male, and the average height of volleyball players is much higher than that of jockeys. Figure 2.6 shows such differences in the definition of fuzzy sets for "moderate" height.

2.1.3 The Notation of Fuzzy Sets

I have shown in 2.1.2 that fuzzy sets can be seen as an extension of ordinary sets. However, we must take care with the notation of fuzzy sets because they contain special uses of symbols appearing in ordinary mathematics. Many first-time learners of fuzzy logic have been confused by the special notation of fuzzy sets. Once the reader grasps the meaning of the symbols, the basics of fuzzy sets can be understood fairly easily.

The methods of expression for fuzzy sets can be roughly divided into two as in the following definitions.

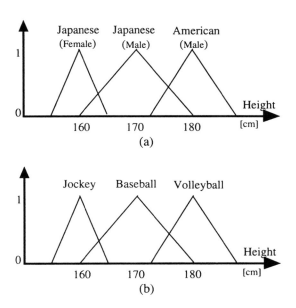

FIGURE 2.6. Fuzzy sets representing moderate height: (a) difference in nationality; (b) difference in sports.

Expression of fuzzy sets

- Discrete expression (when the universe is finite): Let the universe X be

  $X = \{x_1, x_2, \ldots, x_n\}$.

  Then, a fuzzy set A on X can be represented as follows:

  $$A = \mu_A(x_1)/x_1 + \mu_A(x_2)/x_2 + \cdots + \mu_A(x_n)/x_n$$

  $$= \sum_{i=1}^{n} \mu_A(x_i)/x_i \qquad (2.13)$$

- Continuous expression (when the universe is infinite): When the universe X is an infinite set, a fuzzy set A on X can be represented as follows.

  $$A = \int_x \mu_A(x_i)/x_i \qquad (2.14)$$

The symbol / in (2.13) and (2.14) is called a separator. On the right of the separator we write an element of the universe and on the left we write the membership value of the element in the defining set. We write each element in the same fashion, and we connect terms by the + symbol. In ordinary mathematics the symbols / and + mean division and addition respectively, but they are different for the definition of fuzzy sets. If we need to aggregate the terms in the discrete expression, we use the Σ symbol but the meaning of Σ is again different from the normal symbol in mathematics.

There are two other rules for the discrete expression:

i. When the grade of membership for an element x' is zero, that is, $\mu_A(x') = 0$, we do not write $0/x'$ but we can omit the term.

ii. If there are several values assigned to one element of the universe, we can take the maximum value to represent the membership value. For example, for x',

$$0.6/x' + 0.7/x' + 0.3/x'- > 0.7/x'.$$

On the other hand, in a continuous expression, the symbol $\int$ is used as an extension of Σ to the continuous world, and it has no connection with the integral. On the lower right of the $\int$ symbol we write the name of the universe so that it indicates in what universe the fuzzy set is represented. In a continuous expression, there are an infinite number of elements and we cannot write the elements and their membership values. Therefore we put the element as a variable such as x on the right of the separator, and the membership function on the left.

Here I rewrite the definition of the fuzzy set expression in a general form as follows:

Expression of fuzzy sets

- Discrete expression:

  (Membership value of the first element)/(the value of the first element)

      + (Membership value of the second element)/(the value of the second element)

      + ···

      + (Membership value of the nth element)/(the value of the nth element)

  $$= \sum_{i=1}^{n} \text{(Membership value of the } i\text{th element)/(The value of the}$$
      ith element).

- Continuous expression:

  $$\int_{\text{universe}} \text{(Membership function/Element variable)}.$$

There can be an infinite number of variations of fuzzy sets but the practical types are limited. I introduce some of the popular fuzzy sets in the next example.

EXAMPLE 2.5. POPULAR FUZZY SETS

In this example I introduce three different types of fuzzy sets—triangular, trapezoidal, and exponential.

Example 2.5.i. Triangular fuzzy sets
Figures 2.7 and 2.8 show infinite and finite expression of triangular fuzzy sets, respectively, with base 4 and their peak at x = 0.
The infinite expression of the fuzzy set in Figure 2.7 is

$$A = \int_{-2}^{0} \left(\frac{2+x}{2}\right) \Big/ x + \int_{0}^{2} \left(\frac{2-x}{2}\right) \Big/ x.$$

Let us try to rewrite this expression by a finite expression.

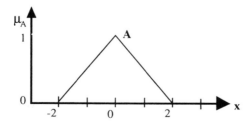

FIGURE 2.7. Infinite expression (triangular).

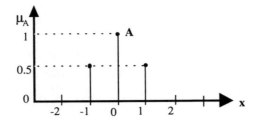

FIGURE 2.8. Finite expression (Case 1).

Case 1.
   If the universe X is given as

$$X = \{-2, -1, 0, 1, 2\},$$
$$A = 0.5/-1 + 1.0/0 + 0.5/1.$$

This is shown in Figure 2.8.

Case 2.
   If the universe X is more complicated as

$$X = \{-2, -1.5, -1, -0.5, 0, 0.5, 1, 1.5, 2\},$$
$$A = 0.25/-1.5 + 0.5/-1 + 0.75/-0.5 + 1.0/0 + +0.75/0.5$$
$$+ 0.5/1 + 0.25/1.5.$$

This is shown in Figure 2.9.

Example 2.5.ii. Trapezoidal fuzzy sets
   Figure 2.10 shows an example of trapezoidal fuzzy sets. This trapezoidal fuzzy set can be expressed by the infinite expression:

$$B = \int_{-4}^{-2} \left(\frac{4+x}{2}\right) /x + \int_{2}^{2} 1/x + \int_{2}^{4} \left(\frac{4-x}{2}\right) /x.$$

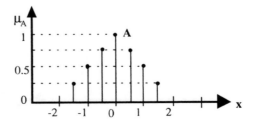

FIGURE 2.9. Finite expression (Case 2).

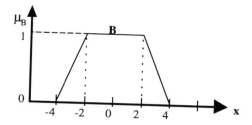

FIGURE 2.10. Trapezoidal fuzzy set.

Next, let us think of finite expression. If the universe X is given as

$$X = \{-5, -4, -3, -2, -1, 0, 1, 2, 3, 4, 5\},$$

the finite expression of the fuzzy set B will be

$$B = 0.5/-3 + 1/-2 + 1/-1 + 1/0 + 1/1 + 1/2 + 0.5/3.$$

Example 2.5.iii. Exponential fuzzy sets

Figure 2.11 shows an example of an exponential fuzzy set. The membership function of this type of fuzzy set is expressed by exponential functions. The infinite expression of this type of fuzzy set can be

$$D = \int_x e^{-0.5(x-5)^2}/x.$$

Now let us consider a finite expression of exponential fuzzy sets. If the universe X is given as

$$X = \{0, 2, 4, 6, 8, 10\},$$

then the finite expression of D will be

$$D = 0.11/2 + 0.607/4 + 0.607/6 + 0.11/8.$$

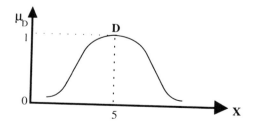

FIGURE 2.11. Exponential fuzzy set.

Because the membership values of elements 0 and 10 are very small and approximated with the value 0, is thus they are omitted from the expression:

$$\mu_D(0) = \mu_D(10) = 3.73 \times 10^{-6} \approx 0.$$

Next, the method of representing fuzzy sets on computer programs is introduced. Discrete expression is more suitable than continuous expression for representation on a computer because fuzzy sets are represented by arrays, as shown in the following. Continuous expression of fuzzy sets can always be approximated by discrete expression and it causes no difficulty if we commit ourselves to discrete expression hereafter.

The problem of discrete expression for originally continuous fuzzy sets is how many elements we assign to the discrete expression. If we assign too few elements, the accuracy of approximating the fuzzy set is not very good. On the other hand, too many elements consume too much memory. Therefore, we need to select a proper number of elements for the discrete expression.

I have mentioned that arrays are effective for the representation of discrete fuzzy sets on computers. There are many other techniques applicable for such representation. However, every method is basically the same in function and I only deal with arrays in this book.

Suppose a fuzzy set A is defined as

$$A = \mu_A(x_1)/X_1 + \mu_A(x_2)/X_2 + \mu_A(x_3)/X_3 + \mu_A(x_4)/X_4 + \mu_A(x_5)/X_5.$$

If we substitute the membership value of this fuzzy set into a C language-like array, we get

	A[0]	A[1]	A[2]	A[3]	A[4]
Name of array A	$\mu_A(x_1)$	$\mu_A(x_2)$	$\mu_A(x_3)$	$\mu_A(x_4)$	$\mu_A(x_5)$

The preceding data represent the array for A on a computer.

The relation between array elements and membership value is

$$A[i - 1] = \mu_A(x_i), \qquad i = 1, 2, 3, 4, 5.$$

EXAMPLE 2.6. REPRESENTATION OF FUZZY SETS ON COMPUTERS

In this example let us represent the exponential fuzzy set introduced in Example 2.5.iii using an array.

The universe X is given as

$$X = \{0, 2, 4, 6, 8, 10\},$$

and the fuzzy set is

$$D = 0.011/2 + 0.607/4 + 0.607/6 + 0.011/8.$$

Substituting the membership value into the array elements one by one, we get

	D[0]	D[1]	D[2]	D[3]	D[4]	D[5]
array name D	0	0.011	0.607	0.607	0.011	0
subscript	0	1	2	3	4	5
The universe X =	{0	2	4	6	8	10}

As in the previous example, the array's subscripts and the elements of the universe are not equal in general. In such a case, we must note the correspondence of the subscripts and the elements of the universe. In this example, for D there are the following relations between the array subscripts and the elements of the universe.

subscript		elements of universe
0	→	0
1	→	2
2	→	4
3	→	6
4	→	8
5	→	10
In general a	→	$2a$

If we assign a to a subscript, the corresponding element of the universe is $2a$. For example, subscript 3 of the array corresponds with the element 6 of the universe. Also, element 8 of the universe corresponds with subscript 4. If we write such correspondence in a general equation,

The element of the universe $= x_{min} + i(x_{max} - x_{min})/(n - 1)$,

where

x_{min} :   the minimum value of the elements of the universe;

x_{max} :   the maximum value of the elements of the universe;

i   :   the subscript of array elements; and

n   :   the number of elements in the universe.

For the preceding equation to be valid, the elements of the universe need to be equal values apart. For example, if the universe X is given as

$X = \{0, 2, 3, 6, 7, 10\}$,

the elements are not apart from each other in the equal value, and we cannot apply the previous equation.

Let us apply the previous equation to array D, then. First of all, we see

$x_{min} = 0$;

$x_{max} = 10$;

$n = 6$.

If the subscript i $= 0$, the corresponding element of the universe can be obtained such that

$$0 + 0 \times \frac{10}{5} = 0.$$

Similarly, if i $= 2$, the corresponding element of the universe is

$$0 + 2 \times \frac{10}{5} = 4.$$

2.1.4 Normal, Convex, and Cardinality of Fuzzy Sets

In this section, I describe normal fuzzy sets, convex fuzzy sets, and the cardinality of a fuzzy set.

Normal, convex, and cardinality

Let A be a fuzzy set on the universe X. A normal fuzzy set, a convex fuzzy set, and the cardinality of a fuzzy set are defined as follows.

- Normal fuzzy set: the fuzzy set A is normal if

$$\max_{x \in X} \mu_A(x) = 1. \tag{2.15}$$

- Convex fuzzy set: the fuzzy set A is convex if

$$\text{for } \forall x_1 \in X, \forall x_2 \in X, \forall \lambda \in [0, 1]$$
$$\mu_A\left(\lambda x_1 + (1 - \lambda)x_2\right) \geq \min\left(\mu_A(x_1), \mu_A(x_2)\right). \tag{2.16}$$

- Cardinality: when X is a finite set, the cardinality of fuzzy set A on X is defined by

$$|A| = \sum_{x \in X} \mu_A(x). \tag{2.17}$$

- Relative cardinality: the relative cardinality of fuzzy set A on X is defined by

$$\|A\| = \frac{|A|}{|X|}, \tag{2.18}$$

where $|A|$ is the cardinality of A and $|X|$ is the cardinality of the universe X.

Equation (2.15) means that if the maximum value of the membership grade equals 1, the fuzzy set A is normal.

Alternatively, we can define a function for the maximum value of μ_A as

$$\text{Height}(A) = \max_{x \in X} \mu_A(x),$$

and if Height $(A) = 1$, the fuzzy set A is normal.

Equation (2.16) for the convex fuzzy set can also be defined as follows. In an arbitrary interval $[x1, x_2]$ for all $x \in [x_1, x_2]$ the following condition holds true,

$$\mu_A(x) \geq \min\left(\mu_A(x_1), \quad \mu_A(x_2)\right),$$

where $\min(a, b)$ is the operator to take smaller value of a or b.

The definition of cardinality for fuzzy sets is an extension of the cardinality for crisp sets. Let us suppose a special membership function such as:

$$\mu_A(x) = \begin{cases} 1 & x \in A \\ 0 & x \notin A \end{cases}.$$

This is a characteristic function of a crisp set. In this case the value of $\sum_{x \in X} \mu_A(x)$ is the number of elements and (2.17) results in the cardinality of crisp sets.

EXAMPLE 2.7. NORMAL, CONVEX, AND CARDINALITY OF FUZZY SETS

Figures 2.12, 2.13, and 2.14 show examples of a normal fuzzy set, a convex fuzzy set, and the cardinality of a fuzzy set, respectively.

The following is a discussion on the judgment of normality and convexity of a fuzzy set from arrays of data. Suppose two fuzzy sets A and B are given by the following arrays.

	A[0]	A[1]	A[2]	A[3]	A[4]	A[5]
Name of array A	0.5	0.9	0.7	1.0	0.7	0.3

	B[0]	B[1]	B[2]	B[3]	B[4]	B[5]
Name of array B	0	0.4	0.8	0.7	0.2	0

To judge if a fuzzy set is normal, we find the maximum value of the array and check if it is equal to 1. Because the maximum value of the array A is 1.0, fuzzy set A is normal. On the other hand, because the maximum value of the array B is 0.8, fuzzy set B is not normal.

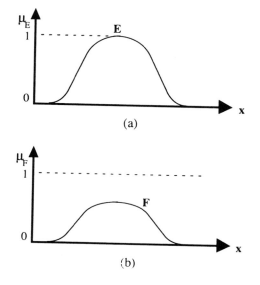

(a)

(b)

FIGURE 2.12. fuzzy sets: (a) normal; (b) not normal.

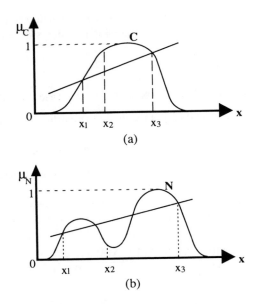

FIGURE 2.13. Fuzzy sets: (a) convex; (b) not convex.

The judgment of convexity is not as straightforward as that of normality. Starting from the first (leftmost) element of the array, we compare the adjacent elements sequentially. We observe the relationship for the first few elements as

$$A[i] < A[i + 1], \qquad i = 0, 1, \ldots.$$

If the preceding inequality no longer holds at an i-th element, we store the subscript i. In the preceding sample array A, we notice that $A[1] > A[2]$. Therefore we store the subscript 1.

Next, from the last (rightmost) element of the array we compare the adjacent elements in the reverse direction. We observe for the first few elements of the

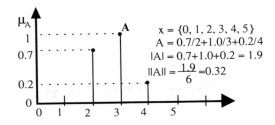

FIGURE 2.14. Cardinality of fuzzy sets.

search the following inequality holds:

A[i] $\geq$ A[i + 1],   i = k, k − 1, k − 2, ...

Here, k is the largest subscript. We then store the subscript i + 1, if this relation no longer holds true for *i*. In array A, we notice that A[2] < A[3], so we store the subscript 3. If the subscripts stored in the preceding operations are the same, the fuzzy set is convex. Inasmuch as the two subscripts are different for array A, fuzzy set A is not convex.

Try to apply the same procedure to array B. We will get the same subscript 2 for both directions of the search, and fuzzy set B is convex.

2.2 Fundamental Operations of Fuzzy Sets—Union, Intersection, and Complement

In this section I introduce union, intersection, and complement of fuzzy sets. These can be derived by operations of their membership functions as defined in the following.

Union, intersection, and complement of fuzzy sets

- Union of fuzzy sets A and B: union A $\cup$ B of fuzzy sets A and B is a fuzzy set defined by the membership function:

$$\mu_{A \cup B}(x) = \mu_A(x) \vee \mu_B(x), \tag{2.19}$$

where

$$\mu_A(x) \vee \mu_B(x) = \begin{cases} \mu_A(x) & \mu_A(x) \geq \mu_B(x) \\ \mu_B(x) & \mu_A(x) < \mu_B(x); \end{cases}$$

$\mu_A(x) \vee \mu_B(x)$ can be written as $\max\{\mu_A(x), \mu_B(x)\}$.

- Intersection of fuzzy sets A and B: intersection A $\cap$ B of fuzzy sets A and B is a fuzzy set defined by the membership function:

$$\mu_{A \cap B}(x) = \mu_A(x) \wedge \mu_B(x), \tag{2.20}$$

where

$$\mu_A(x) \wedge \mu_B(x) = \begin{cases} \mu_A(x) & \mu_A(x) \leq \mu_B(x) \\ \mu_B(x) & \mu_A(x) > \mu_B(x); \end{cases}$$

$\mu_A(x) \wedge \mu_B(x)$ can be written as $\min\{\mu_A(x), \mu_B(x)\}$.

- Complement of fuzzy set A: complement $\overline{A}$ of fuzzy set A is a fuzzy set defined by the membership function:

$$\mu_{\overline{A}}(x) = 1 - \mu_A(x). \tag{2.21}$$

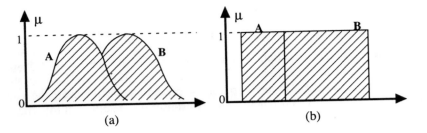

FIGURE 2.15. Union: (a) fuzzy sets; (b) crisp sets.

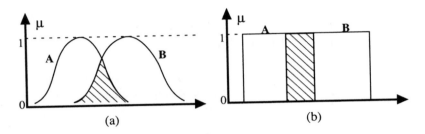

FIGURE 2.16. Intersection: (a) fuzzy sets; (b) crisp sets.

Note that union, intersection, and complement of crisp sets are special cases of union, intersection, and complement of fuzzy sets, respectively. Therefore, by replacing membership functions with characteristic equations we can derive fundamental operations of crisp sets.

EXAMPLE 2.8. UNION, INTERSECTION, AND COMPLEMENT OF FUZZY SETS

Figures 2.15, 2.16, 2.17 show examples of union, intersection, and complements of fuzzy sets. The membership functions of the union, intersection, and complement are derived from the definitions (2.19) through (2.21).

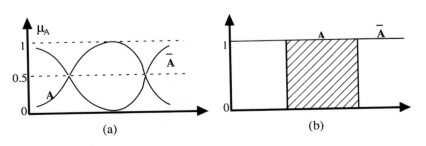

FIGURE 2.17. Complement: (a) fuzzy sets; (b) crisp sets.

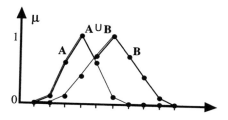

FIGURE 2.18. Union of A and B.

Now I show how to calculate union, intersection, and complement on computers. I have mentioned that finite fuzzy sets can be represented by arrays. Therefore, union, intersection, and complement are given by operations of arrays.

Let fuzzy sets A and B be expressed in the following arrays.

A	0	0.1	0.6	1.0	0.6	0.1	0	0	0	0
B	0	0	0.1	0.4	0.7	1.0	0.7	0.4	0.1	0

To calculate union A ∪ B we compare each corresponding element of the arrays and substitute the largest value of the two into another array representing A ∪ B. For the preceding A and B we get

A ∪ B	0	0.1	0.6	1.0	0.7	1.0	0.7	0.4	0.1	0

Figure 2.18 shows this operation.

On the other hand, to calculate intersection A ∩ B we substitute the smallest value of the corresponding elements into another array representing A ∩ B such that:

A	0	0.1	0.6	1.0	0.6	0.1	0	0	0	0
B	0	0	0.1	0.4	0.7	1.0	0.7	0.4	0.1	0
A ∩ B	0	0	0.1	0.4	0.6	0.1	0	0	0	0

Figure 2.19 indicates this operation.

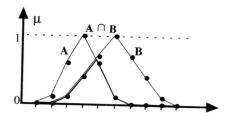

FIGURE 2.19. Intersection of A and B.

Complements can be obtained by subtracting the value of each element from 1. The array of $\overline{A}$ is given as follows.

A	0	0.1	0.6	1.0	0.6	0.1	0	0	0	0
$\overline{A}$	1.0	0.9	0.4	0	0.4	0.9	1.0	1.0	1.0	1.0

Figure 2.20 shows such an operation.

The principle operations of fuzzy sets have the following properties. Some properties are valid for both fuzzy and crisp sets. Other properties are valid for crisp sets only.

Properties of fuzzy sets

Let A, B, and C be fuzzy sets on the universe X.

i. Properties valid for both fuzzy and crisp sets.

- Idempotent law:

$$A \cup A = A, \qquad A \cap A = A. \tag{2.22}$$

- Communicative law:

$$A \cup B = B \cup A, \qquad A \cap B = B \cap A. \tag{2.23}$$

- Associative law:

$$A \cup (B \cup C) = (A \cup B) \cup C,$$
$$A \cap (B \cap C) = (A \cap B) \cap C. \tag{2.24}$$

- Distributive law:

$$A \cup (B \cap C) = (A \cup B) \cap (A \cup C),$$
$$A \cap (B \cup C) = (A \cap B) \cup (A \cap C). \tag{2.25}$$

- The law of double negation:

$$A = \overline{\overline{A}}. \tag{2.26}$$

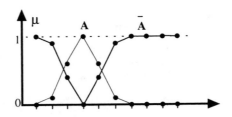

FIGURE 2.20. Complement of A.

- De Morgan's law:

$$\overline{A \cup B} = \overline{A} \cap \overline{B},$$

$$\overline{A \cap B} = \overline{A} \cup \overline{B}. \tag{2.27}$$

ii. Properties valid for crisp sets, but in general not valid for fuzzy sets.

- The law of excluded middle:

$$A \cup \overline{A} \neq X. \tag{2.28}$$

- The law of contradiction:

$$A \cap \overline{A} \neq \varnothing, \tag{2.29}$$

where $\varnothing$ means an empty set.

The laws of excluded middle and contradiction do not hold valid for general fuzzy sets.

EXAMPLE 2.9. LAWS OF EXCLUDED MIDDLE AND CONTRADICTION

In this example I show examples of the laws of the excluded middle and contradiction, which do not hold true in fuzzy sets. Figure 2.21 indicates the law of excluded middle and Figure 2.22 shows the law of contradiction.

Next I introduce equality and inclusion of fuzzy sets.

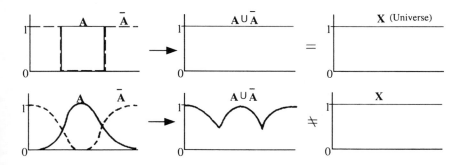

FIGURE 2.21. The law of excluded middle.

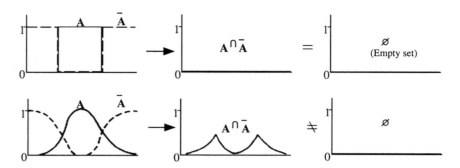

FIGURE 2.22. Law of contradiction.

Equality and inclusion of fuzzy sets

Let A and B be fuzzy sets on the universe X.

- Equality of fuzzy sets: the equality of fuzzy sets A and B is defined as

$$A = B \Leftrightarrow \mu_A(x) = \mu_B(x), \qquad \forall_x x \in X. \tag{2.30}$$

- Inclusion of fuzzy sets: the inclusion of fuzzy set A in B, or A being a subset of B, is defined as

$$A \subset B \Leftrightarrow \mu_A(x) \leq \mu_B(x), \qquad \forall x \in X \tag{2.31}$$

Fuzzy sets A and B are equal when their membership values are identical. Similarly, A is included in B when all the membership values of fuzzy set B are equal to or larger than the corresponding membership values of A.

Figures 2.23 and 2.24 show equality and inclusion, respectively.

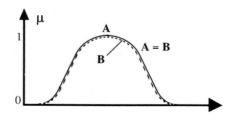

FIGURE 2.23. Equality.

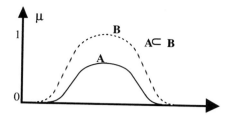

FIGURE 2.24. Inclusion.

The following is a description of how to judge equality and inclusion by computers. Suppose arrays to represent fuzzy sets A and B are given as follows.

A	0	0.1	0.6	1.0	0.6	0.1	0	0	0	0
B	0	0.1	0.6	1.0	0.6	0.1	0	0	0	0

To judge the equality of the preceding fuzzy sets we compare each corresponding element and check if they are equal.

In the case of preceding arrays, we notice

$$A[i] = B[i], \qquad i = 0, \dots, 9.$$

Therefore $A = B$.

Next, suppose fuzzy sets A and B are given as follows.

A	0	0.1	0.6	1.0	0.6	0.1	0	0	0	0
B	0	0.1	0.6	1.0	0.8	0.1	0	0	0	0

In this case, $A[4] \neq B[4]$ and then $A \neq B$.

As shown in this example, if even one pair of membership values are not equal, equality does not hold.

Let us see the inclusion of fuzzy sets A and B. To judge inclusion $A \subset B$, we compare corresponding elements and see if the values of elements in B are equal to or greater than those of A. Consider the arrays:

A	0	0.1	0.5	0.9	0.5	0	0	0	0	0
B	0	0.1	0.6	1.0	0.6	0.1	0	0	0	0

When we compare these arrays, we find

$$A[i] \leq B[i], \qquad i = 0, \dots, 9.$$

Therefore $A \subset B$.

However, if A and B are

A	0	0.1	0.5	0.9	0.9	0	0	0	0	0
B	0	0.1	0.6	1.0	0.6	0.1	0	0	0	0

$$A[4] > B[4].$$

Then $A \not\subset B$.

2.3 α-Cuts and Decomposition Principle

In this section, I explain α-cuts and the decomposition principle based on the idea of α-cuts.

α-cuts and decomposition principle

Consider a fuzzy set A on the universe X.

- α-cuts: for the fuzzy set A we can define the following α-cuts.

$$\text{strong } \alpha\text{-cut:} \quad A_\alpha = \{x \mid \mu_A(x) > \alpha\}, \quad \alpha \in [0, 1) \tag{2.32}$$

$$\text{weak } \alpha\text{-cut:} \quad A_{\bar{\alpha}} = \{x \mid \mu_A(x) \geq \alpha\}, \quad \alpha \in (0, 1] \tag{2.33}$$

Weak α-cuts are sometimes called α-level sets.

- Decomposition principle: using α-cuts we can decompose a membership function $\mu_A(x)$ into an infinite number of rectangular membership functions ($\alpha \wedge \chi_{A_\alpha}(x)$ or $\alpha \wedge \chi_{A_{\bar{\alpha}}}(x)$). When we aggregate these rectangular membership functions and apply max-operation, the original fuzzy set A can be obtained:

$$\mu_A(x) = \max_{\alpha \in [0,1)} \left[\alpha \wedge \chi_{A_\alpha}(x) \right] = \max_{\alpha \in (0,1]} \left[\alpha \wedge \chi_{A_{\bar{\alpha}}}(x) \right] \tag{2.34}$$

Here, $\chi_{A_\alpha}(x)$ is a characteristic equation of the set A_α.

The difference between strong and weak α-cuts centers on whether they include equality.

Figure 2.25 shows an example of an α-cut.

Figure 2.26 illustrates the idea of the decomposition principle. Let the characteristic function of a weak α-cut $\chi_{A_{\bar{\alpha}}}(x)$ for an α ($\alpha \in (0, 1]$). Define a rectangular membership function that satisfies $\alpha \wedge \chi_{A_{\bar{\alpha}}}(x)$. Changing the value of α in the interval of $\alpha \in (0, 1]$ we repeat the similar operation and get an infinite number of rectangular membership functions. The decomposition principle tells us that the

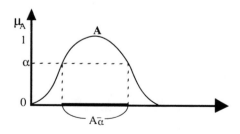

FIGURE 2.25. α-cut.

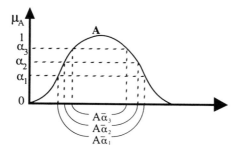

FIGURE 2.26. Decomposition principle.

membership function of the original fuzzy set A can be expressed by the max-operation of the previously obtained rectangular membership functions. This is defined by

$$\mu_A(x) = \max_{\alpha \in (0,1]} \left[\alpha \wedge \chi_{A_{\bar{\alpha}}}(x) \right].$$

EXAMPLE 2.10. DECOMPOSITION PRINCIPLE

Suppose a fuzzy set A defined by the discrete expression:

$$A = 0.2/1 + 0.5/2 + 0.7/3 + 1.0/4 + 0.8/5 + 0.4/6 + 0.2/7.$$

If we apply weak α-cuts for $\alpha \in (0, 1]$ from 0.1 to 1 with the step width of 0.1, we get the following α-cuts.

$$A_{\overline{0.1}} = A_{\overline{0.2}} = \{1, 2, 3, 4, 5, 6, 7\}$$
$$A_{\overline{0.3}} = A_{\overline{0.4}} = \{2, 3, 4, 5, 6\}$$
$$A_{\overline{0.5}} = \{2, 3, 4, 5\}$$
$$A_{\overline{0.6}} = A_{\overline{0.7}} = \{3, 4, 5\}$$
$$A_{\overline{0.8}} = \{4, 5\}$$
$$A_{\overline{0.9}} = A_{\overline{1.0}} = \{4\}.$$

Now let us try to reconstruct the fuzzy set A using these α-cuts. First, we rewrite the α-cuts by discrete expression of fuzzy sets as follows.

$$A_{\overline{0.1}} = 1.0/1 + 1.0/2 + 1.0/3 + 1.0/4 + 1.0/5 + 1.0/6 + 1.0/7$$
$$A_{\overline{0.2}} = 1.0/1 + 1.0/2 + 1.0/3 + 1.0/4 + 1.0/5 + 1.0/6 + 1.0/7$$
$$A_{\overline{0.3}} = 1.0/2 + 1.0/3 + 1.0/4 + 1.0/5 + 1.0/6$$
$$A_{\overline{0.4}} = 1.0/2 + 1.0/3 + 1.0/4 + 1.0/5 + 1.0/6$$
$$A_{\overline{0.5}} = 1.0/2 + 1.0/3 + 1.0/4 + 1.0/5$$
$$A_{\overline{0.6}} = 1.0/3 + 1.0/4 + 1.0/5$$

$$A_{\overline{0.7}} = 1.0/3 + 1.0/4 + 1.0/5$$
$$A_{\overline{0.8}} = 1.0/4 + 1.0/5$$
$$A_{\overline{0.9}} = 1.0/4$$
$$A_{\overline{1.0}} = 1.0/4.$$

Here, because $A_{\overline{0.1}}$ is given as

$$A_{\overline{0.1}} = \{1, 2, 3, 4, 5, 6, 7\},$$

when we assign the value 1.0 of the characteristic equation for these elements, we get

$$A_{\overline{0.1}} = 1.0/1 + 1.0/2 + 1.0/3 + 1.0/4 + 1.0/5 + 1.0/6 + 1.0/7.$$

Similar operation derives the preceding expression from $A_{\overline{0.2}}$ to $A_{\overline{1.0}}$. If we focus on the value of the characteristic equation, we notice that

$$\chi_{A_{\overline{\alpha}}}(1) = \cdots = \chi_{A_{\overline{\alpha}}}(7) = 1.0.$$

Next, we calculate $\alpha \wedge \chi_{A_{\overline{\alpha}}}(x)$.
    Assume

$$x_1 = 1, x_2 = 2, \ldots, X_7 = 7$$

or

$$X_i = i \quad \text{for } i = 1, \ldots, 7.$$

If we denote a fuzzy set $A_{\overline{\alpha}}^*$ that has $\alpha \wedge \chi_{A_{\overline{\alpha}}}(x)$ as the membership value, we can calculate $A_{\overline{\alpha}}^*$ as follows.

$$A_{\overline{0.1}}^* = \sum_{i=1}^{7} \left(\left[0.1 \wedge \chi_{A_{\overline{0.1}}}(x_i) \right] \Big/ x_i \right)$$
$$= \left[0.1 \wedge \chi_{A0.1}(x_1) \right] \Big/ x_1 + \cdots + \left[0.1 \wedge \chi_{A_{\overline{0.1}}}(x_7) \right] \Big/ x_7$$
$$= \left[0.1 \wedge \chi_{A_{\overline{0.1}}}(x_1) \right] \Big/ 1 + \cdots + \left[0.1 \wedge \chi_{A_{\overline{0.1}}}(x_7) \right] \Big/ 7$$
$$= 0.1/1 + 0.1/2 + 0.1/3 + 0.1/4 + 0.1/5 + 0.1/6 + 0.1/7$$

$$A_{\overline{0.2}}^* = \sum_{i=1}^{7} \left(\left[0.1 \wedge \chi_{A_{\overline{0.2}}}(x_i) \right] \Big/ x_i \right)$$
$$= 0.2/1 + 0.2/2 + 0.2/3 + 0.2/4 + 0.2/5 + 0.2/6 + 0.2/7$$

$$A_{\overline{0.3}}^* = \sum_{i=1}^{7} \left(\left[0.1 \wedge \chi_{A_{\overline{0.3}}}(x_i) \right] \Big/ x_i \right)$$
$$= 0.3/2 + 0.3/3 + 0.3/4 + 0.3/5 + 0.3/6$$

$$A^*_{\overline{0.4}} = \sum_{i=1}^{7} \left(\left[0.1 \wedge \chi_{A_{\overline{0.4}}}(x_i) \right] \Big/ x_i \right)$$

$$= 0.4/2 + 0.4/3 + 0.4/4 + 0.4/5 + 0.4/6$$

$$A^*_{\overline{0.5}} = \sum_{i=1}^{7} \left(\left[0.1 \wedge \chi_{A_{\overline{0.5}}}(x_i) \right] \Big/ x_i \right)$$

$$= 0.5/2 + 0.5/3 + 0.5/4 + 0.5/5$$

$$A^*_{\overline{0.6}} = \sum_{i=1}^{7} \left(\left[0.1 \wedge \chi_{A_{\overline{0.6}}}(x_i) \right] \Big/ x_i \right)$$

$$= 0.6/3 + 0.6/4 + 0.6/5$$

$$A^*_{\overline{0.7}} = \sum_{i=1}^{7} \left(\left[0.1 \wedge \chi_{A_{\overline{0.7}}}(x_i) \right] \Big/ x_i \right)$$

$$= 0.7/3 + 0.7/4 + 0.7/5$$

$$A^*_{\overline{0.8}} = \sum_{i=1}^{7} \left(\left[0.1 \wedge \chi_{A_{\overline{0.8}}}(x_i) \right] \Big/ x_i \right)$$

$$= 0.8/4 + 0.8/5$$

$$A^*_{\overline{0.9}} = \sum_{i=1}^{7} \left(\left[0.1 \wedge \chi_{A_{\overline{0.9}}}(x_i) \right] \Big/ x_i \right)$$

$$= 0.9/4$$

$$A^*_{\overline{1.0}} = \sum_{i=1}^{7} \left(\left[0.1 \wedge \chi_{A_{\overline{1.0}}}(x_i) \right] \Big/ x_i \right)$$

$$= 1.0/4.$$

Calculating the union of the preceding fuzzy sets, we get the original fuzzy set A such that

$$\bigcup_{\alpha \in (0,1]} A^*_\alpha = \bigcup_{\alpha \in (0,1]} \left\{ \sum_{i=1}^{7} \left(\left[\alpha \wedge \chi_{A_{\overline{\alpha}}}(x_i) \right] \Big/ x_i \right) \right\}$$

$$= 0.2/1 + 0.5/2 + 0.7/3 + 1.0/4 + 0.8/5 + 0.4/6 + 0.2/7$$

$$= A.$$

This can also be written as

$$\mu_A(x) = \max_{\alpha \in (0,1]} \left[\alpha \wedge \chi_{A_{\overline{\alpha}}}(x) \right].$$

The preceding expression is the same as (2.34).

In this example, the resolution of membership values is 0.1 and it is sufficient to represent the fuzzy set A by α-cuts. For a continuous fuzzy set, max-operation should more precisely be applied for the interval of $\alpha \in (0, 1]$.

The following discussion is about how to realize α-cuts on computers. Suppose a fuzzy set is given in an array such as

	A[0]	A[1]	A[2]	A[3]	A[4]	A[5]	A[6]	A[7]	A[8]
A	0	0.1	0.6	1.0	0.5	0.1	0	0	0

The α-cuts are calculated by processing elements of A so that

if $\alpha < A[i]$, $A[i] = 1$, $i = 0, 1, \ldots, 7, 8$;

otherwise, $A[i] = 0$;

for an α which gives a weak α-cut.

For example, for $\alpha=0.2$, $\alpha=0.6$, and $\alpha=0.8$, resultant arrays will be

$A_{\overline{0.2}}$	0	0	1.0	1.0	1.0	0	0	0	0
$A_{\overline{0.6}}$	0	0	1.0	1.0	0	0	0	0	0
$A_{\overline{0.8}}$	0	0	0	1.0	0	0	0	0	0

2.4 Fuzzy Numbers and the Extension Principle

Section 2.4.1 introduces the extension principle and Section 2.4.2 describes operations of fuzzy numbers using the extension principle. Section 2.4.3 describes L-R fuzzy numbers and their calculation formula.

2.4.1 Extension Principle

By introducing the extension principle we can define various operations of fuzzy sets.

When there is a relation $y = 3x + 2$ between x and y, the value of y for $x = 4$ can be calculated by

$3 \times 4 + 2 = 14.$

Then, how can we calculate the value of y when x is given by a fuzzy set such as $x = $ "about 4?" The extension principle gives a method for doing this.

Figure 2.27 shows the idea of the extension principle. The process of calculation in Figure 2.27 can be interpreted as

$3 \times$ "about 4" $+ 2 = $ "about 12" $+ 2 = $ "about 14."

Now I introduce necessary ideas to explain the extension principle. Consider a mapping from a set X to another set Y such as

$f : X \rightarrow Y.$

Here, let A be a subset of X. Then

$f(A) = \{y \mid y = f(x), x \in A\}$

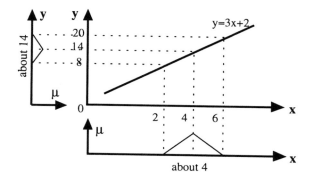

FIGURE 2.27. The concept of the extension principle.

is called the image of A by f. Note that f(A) is a subset of Y.
Similarly, let B be a subset of Y. Then

$$f^{-1}(B) = \{x \mid f(x) = y, y \in B\}$$

is called an inverse image of B by f. $f^{-1}(B)$ is a subset of X.
Those relations are defined for fuzzy sets A and B by the extension principle given as follows.

Extension principle

Extend mapping $f : X \rightarrow Y$ to relate fuzzy set A on X to fuzzy set B on Y:

$$\mu_{f(A)}(y) = \begin{cases} \sup\limits_{y=f(x)} \mu_A(x) & f^{-1}(y) \neq \varnothing \\ 0 & f^{-1}(y) = \varnothing. \end{cases} \tag{2.35}$$

When f is a one-to-one mapping, we can write the preceding relation simply:

$$\mu_{f(A)}(y) = \mu_A(x). \tag{2.36}$$

EXAMPLE 2.11. EXTENSION PRINCIPLE

Let us analyze the process of the previous example

3 × "about 4" + 2 = "about 12" + 2 = "about 14"

using fuzzy sets and the extension principle.
First of all, consider the mapping given by

$$y = 3x + 2.$$

Let A be the fuzzy set that gives "about 4" such as

$$A = 0.5/3 + 1.0/4 + 0.5/5.$$

Also, define $x_1 = 3$, $x_2 = 4$, $x_3 = 5$ so that

$$y_i = 3x_i + 2, \qquad i = 1, 2, 3.$$

Because f gives the mapping of 1:1, we can apply (2.36) to get $f(A)$ for the fuzzy set A as follows.

$$f(A) = \sum_{i=1}^{3} \mu_{f(A)}(y_i)/y_i$$

$$= \sum_{i=1}^{3} \mu_A(y_i)/(3x_i + 2)$$

$$= 0.5/(3 \times 3 + 2) + 1.0/(3 \times 4 + 2) + 0.5/(3 \times 5 + 2)$$

$$= 0.5/11 + 1.0/14 + 0.5/17$$

$$= \text{"about 14."}$$

Because $f(A)$ is a symmetrical fuzzy set with the membership value of 1 at 14, we can interpret this fuzzy set as "about 14."

Let us extend the preceding discussion to a general case. I introduce an idea of Cartesian product used in the definition of the extension principle.

Cartesian product

- Cartesian product: let $x_1, \ldots, x_n$ be the elements of $X_1, \ldots, X_n$. The set of all combinations of $(x_1, \ldots, x_n)$ is called the Cartesian product of $X_1, \ldots, X_n$ and is denoted by $X_1 \times \cdots \times X_n$.

- Cartesian product of fuzzy sets: let $X_1 \times \cdots \times X_n$ be the Cartesian product of the universe $X_1, \ldots, X_n$, and $A_1, \ldots, A_n$ fuzzy sets on $X_1, \ldots, X_n$. The Cartesian product of the fuzzy sets $A_1, \ldots, A_n$ can be defined by

$$A_1 \times \cdots \times A_n$$

$$= \int_{X_1 \times \cdots \times X_n} \min\left(\mu_{A_1}(x_1), \cdots, \mu_{A_n}(x_n)\right)/(x_1, \cdots, x_n) \qquad (2.37)$$

on the universe $X_1 \times \cdots \times X_n$.

The following is the generalized extension principle.

Extension principle (on Cartesian product space)

Let f be a mapping from $X_1 \times \cdots \times X_n$ to Y to satisfy $y = f(x_1, \ldots, x_n)$.

Extending the function f,

$$f : X_1 \times \cdots \times X_n \rightarrow Y,$$

we get the relation between the Cartesian product $A_1 \times \cdots \times A_n$ of fuzzy sets $A_1, \ldots, A_n$ on X and a fuzzy set $B(= f(A_1 \times \cdots \times A_n))$ on Y such that

$$\mu_B(y) = \begin{cases} \sup\limits_{\substack{(x_1,\ldots,x_n)\in \\ X_1\times\ldots\times X_n}} \min\left(\mu_{A_1}(x_1), \ldots, \mu_{A_n}(x_n)\right) & f^{-1}(y) \neq \varnothing \\ 0 & f^{-1}(y) = \varnothing, \end{cases} \tag{2.38}$$

where $f^{-1}(y)$ means the inverse image of y.

2.4.2 Fuzzy Numbers and Their Operations

Fuzzy numbers are fuzzy sets with special consideration for easy calculations. We can define operations of fuzzy numbers using the extension principle. I first give the definition of fuzzy numbers.

Fuzzy numbers

- Fuzzy numbers: if a fuzzy set A on the universe R of real numbers satisfies the following conditions, we call it a fuzzy number.

  i. A is a convex fuzzy set;

  ii. there is only one x_0 that satisfies $\mu_A(x_0) = 1$; and

  iii. μ_A is continuous in an interval.

- Flat fuzzy numbers: if a fuzzy number A satisfies the following condition, we call it a flat fuzzy number.

  $(m_1, m_2) \in R \quad m_1 < m_2$

  $\mu_A(x) = 1 \qquad \forall x \in [m_1, m_2].$ \hfill (2.39)

Condition (iii) of the fuzzy number poses no problem to applications. The difference between flat fuzzy numbers and other fuzzy numbers is whether the element(s) giving the membership value of 1 is given by a point or an interval. Figures 2.28 and 2.29 show examples of fuzzy numbers and a flat fuzzy number, respectively.

Now I introduce the operations of fuzzy numbers based on the extension principle. By applying the extension principle, we obtain a "fuzzy" calculation such as "about 2" plus "about 3" is "about 5".

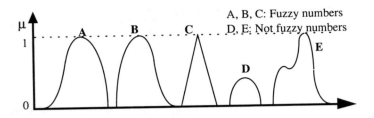

FIGURE 2.28. Fuzzy numbers.

Operation of fuzzy numbers based on the extension principle

The binary operation ∗ of real numbers can be extended to fuzzy numbers A and B on the universe X such as

$$\mu_{A\circledast B}(z) = \sup_{x \ast y} \left[\mu_A(x) \wedge \mu_B(y) \right]. \tag{2.40}$$

If we rewrite the preceding expression using fuzzy sets, we get

$$A \circledast B = \int_{X \times X} \left[\mu_A(x) \wedge \mu_B(y) \right] \Big/ (x \ast y),$$

where

$$x, y, z \in X.$$

Using the preceding definition we can derive the arithmetic of fuzzy numbers as in the following.

Arithmetic of fuzzy numbers

- Addition:

$$\mu_{A\oplus B}(z) = \sup_{x+y} \left[\mu_A(x) \wedge \mu_B \right]. \tag{2.41}$$

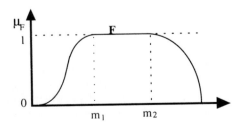

FIGURE 2.29. Flat fuzzy number.

- Subtraction:

$$\mu_{A \ominus B}(z) = \sup_{x-y} \left[\mu_A(x) \wedge \mu_B(y) \right]. \tag{2.42}$$

- Multiplication:

$$\mu_{A \oplus B}(z) = \sup_{x \times y} \left[\mu_A(x) \wedge \mu_B \right]. \tag{2.43}$$

- Division:

$$\mu_{A \oslash B}(z) = \sup_{x+y} \left[\mu_A(x) \wedge \mu_B(y) \right]. \tag{2.44}$$

If an α-cut of a fuzzy set gives a closed interval, we can replace the preceding arithmetic of fuzzy numbers with operations of intervals.

$$[a, b] * [c, d] = \{z \mid z = x * y, x \in [a, b], y \in [c, d]\}$$

When we choose $+$ or $-$ for the operation $*$, we get

$$[a, b] + [c, d] = [a + c, b + d]$$
$$[a, b] - [c, d] = [a - d, b - c]$$

For example,

$$[3, 5] + [4, 8] = [7, 13]$$
$$[3, 5] - [4, 8] = [-5, 1].$$

Although multiplication and division cannot be written in a general form as addition and subtraction, if we assume $a, b, c, d > 0$, we can write

$$[a, b] \times [c, d] = [a \times c, b \times d].$$
$$[a, b] \div [c, d] = [a \div d, b \div c].$$

For example,

$$[3, 5] \times [4, 8] = [12, 40]$$
$$[3, 5] \div [4, 8] = [0.375, 1.25].$$

Note that in fuzzy numbers subtraction is not an inverse operation of addition, and that division is not an inverse operation of multiplication. For example, if we subtract from a number the same number, the result is not zero but a fuzzy number "about 0."

EXAMPLE 2.12. FUZZY NUMBER OPERATIONS USING THE EXTENSION PRINCIPLE

Figure 2.30 shows an example of addition of fuzzy numbers "about 2" and "about 3."

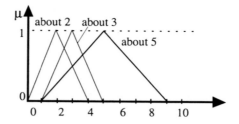

FIGURE 2.30. Addition of fuzzy numbers.

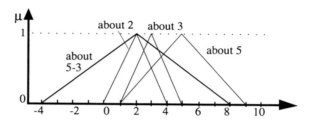

FIGURE 2.31. Subtraction of fuzzy numbers (1).

From the result of this operation we notice that the fuzzy number obtained from the calculation of fuzzy numbers has an increased degree of fuzziness. (Note that the base of the resultant fuzzy number is wider than the original fuzzy numbers.)

EXAMPLE 2.13. SUBTRACTION OF FUZZY NUMBERS (1)

Let us then calculate "about 5" minus "about 3." Figure 2.31 shows the result.
As we can see from the comparison of Figures 2.30 and 2.31, the result of subtraction "about 5"⊖ "about 3" is not "about 2."

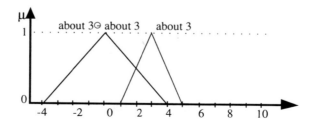

FIGURE 2.32. Subtraction of fuzzy numbers (2).

EXAMPLE 2.14. SUBTRACTION OF FUZZY NUMBERS (2)

Figure 2.32 shows "about 3" minus "about 3." As we can see from Figure 2.32, "about 3" $\ominus$ "about 3" is not zero but "about 0," which is a fuzzy number.

2.4.3 L-R Fuzzy Numbers and Computation Formulas

Dubois and Prade [2] showed that L-R fuzzy numbers achieve high efficiency of calculation. In this section I describe major operations of L-R fuzzy numbers. The definition of L-R fuzzy numbers is given in the following.

L-R fuzzy number

Consider functions L and R that satisfy the conditions:

i. $L(x) = L(-x), \quad R(x) = R(-x)$;

ii. $L(0) = 1, \quad R(0) = 1$;

iii. both L and R are not increasing functions.

L-R fuzzy number M is then defined by L and R such as

$$\mu_M(x) = \begin{cases} L\left(\dfrac{m-x}{\alpha}\right) & x \le m, \alpha > 0 \\ R\left(\dfrac{m-x}{\beta}\right) & x \ge m, \beta > 0. \end{cases}$$

Here, L and R are called *shape functions*, and m is called the *mean value*. α and β define the length of the base in the triangular fuzzy set M to the left and to the right of the mean value, respectively.

Functions L and R can be of any type as long as they satisfy the preceding conditions (i)–(iii). Typical functions are, for example:

$$L(x) = R(x) = \max(0, 1 - |x|^p) \qquad p \ge 0;$$
$$L(x) = R(x) = e^{-|x|^p} \qquad\qquad p \ge 0;$$
$$L(x) = R(x) = 1/(1 + |x|^p) \qquad p \ge 0.$$

Figure 2.33 shows an example of an L-R fuzzy number. Here I have chosen

$$m = 10, \quad \alpha = 1, \quad \beta = 2$$
$$L(x) = \max(0, 1 - |x|)$$
$$R(x) = \max(0, 1 - |x|).$$

The following discussion is on the simplified notation of L-R fuzzy numbers.

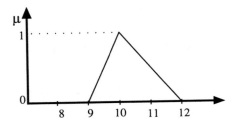

FIGURE 2.33. L-R fuzzy number.

Simple expression of L-R fuzzy numbers

L-R fuzzy number is defined by shape functions $L(x)$ and $R(x)$, mean value m, and parameters α and β, that define the range of the fuzzy number, using the simplified notation

$$M = (m, \alpha, \beta)_{LR}.$$

Figure 2.34 shows the L-R fuzzy number $M = (1, 2, 1)_{LR}$. Here, I use

$$L(x) = \max(0, 1 - |x|)$$
$$R(x) = \max(0, 1 - |x|)$$

for $L(x)$ and $R(x)$.

The next discussion concerns the operations involving L-R fuzzy numbers using simplified expressions. Note that depending on the operation, LR may be replaced by RL. Also, the definition of M for $M > 0$ is

$$\mu_M(x) = 0 \quad \forall x < 0.$$

On the other hand, the definition of M for $M < 0$ is

$$\mu_M(x) = 0 \quad \forall x > 0.$$

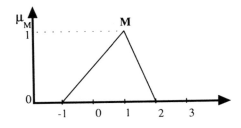

FIGURE 2.34. L-R fuzzy number $M = (1, 2, 1)_{LR}$.

Operations of L-R fuzzy numbers

- Addition:

  $(m, \alpha, \beta)_{LR} \oplus (n, \gamma, \delta)_{LR} = (m + n, \alpha + \gamma, \beta + \delta)_{LR}.$

- Subtraction:

  $(m, \alpha, \beta)_{LR} \ominus (n, \gamma, \delta)_{RL} = (m - n, \alpha + \gamma, \beta + \delta)_{LR}.$

  From the preceding definition we can derive the following relation,

  $-(m, \alpha, \beta)_{LR} = (-m, \beta, \alpha)_{RL}.$

- Multiplication:

  For $M > 0$ and $N > 0$,

  $(m, \alpha, \beta)_{LR} \otimes (n, \gamma, \delta)_{LR} \approx (mn, n\alpha + m\gamma, n\beta + m\delta)_{LR}.$

  For $M < 0$ and $N > 0$,

  $(m, \alpha, \beta)_{LR} \otimes (n, \gamma, \delta)_{LR} \approx (mn, n\alpha - m\delta, n\beta - m\gamma)_{RL}.$

  For $M < 0$ and $N < 0$,

  $(m, \alpha, \beta)_{LR} \otimes (n, \gamma, \delta)_{LR} \approx (mn, -n\beta - m\delta, -n\alpha - m\gamma)_{RL}.$

  From the preceding definitions we can derive the following.

  For $\lambda > 0$,

  $\lambda \otimes (m, \alpha, \beta)_{LR} = (\lambda m, \lambda \alpha, \lambda \beta)_{LR}.$

  For $\lambda < 0$,

  $\lambda \otimes (m, \alpha, \beta)_{LR} = (\lambda m, -\lambda \beta, -\lambda \alpha)_{RL}.$

- Inversion:

  $(m, \alpha, \beta)_{LR}^{-1} \approx (m^{-1}, -\beta m^{-2}, -\alpha m^2)_{RL}.$

- Division:

  For $M > 0$ and $N > 0$,

  $(m, \alpha, \beta)_{LR} \oslash (n, \gamma, \delta)_{RL} \approx \left(\dfrac{m}{m}, \dfrac{m\delta + n\alpha}{n^2}, \dfrac{m\gamma + n\beta}{n^2} \right)_{LR}.$

  The preceding calculation is derived by an approximation of

  $M \oslash N = M \otimes N^{-1}.$

  A similar formula can be obtained for M, N other than $M > 0$ and $N > 0$.

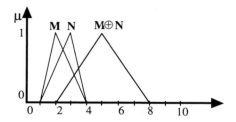

FIGURE 2.35. Addition of L-R fuzzy numbers.

EXAMPLE 2.15. OPERATIONS OF L-R FUZZY NUMBERS

Following is an example of L-R fuzzy numbers. Let fuzzy numbers M, N,

$M = (2, 1, 2)_{LR}$

$N = (3, 2, 1)_{LR}.$

The shape functions are defined as

$L(x) = \max(0, 1 - |x|),$

$R(x) = \max(0, 1 - |x|).$

Applying the preceding addition formula we get

$M \oplus N = (2, 1, 2)_{LR} \oplus (3, 2, 1)_{LR}$

$= (5, 3, 3)_{LR}.$

Figure 2.35 shows the result of this operation. When we represent the operations of L-R fuzzy numbers on computers, we need to determine the values:

  i. mean value;
 ii. parameters α and β; and
iii. shape functions L and R.

2.5 Application Examples of Fuzzy Sets

2.5.1 Matchmaking (1)

In this example, let us consider a computer-assisted matchmaking process for marriage using fuzzy sets.

Suppose a client A of this matchmaking business has this ideal for a partner:

"Neither young nor old; annual income of several thousand US
dollars or more."

There are three potential candidates for the marriage—B, C, and D. A database tells us their age and income:

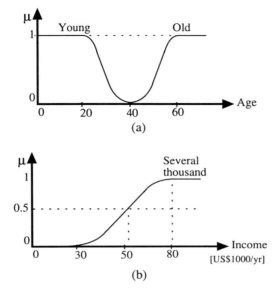

FIGURE 2.36. Fuzzy sets for (a) age and (b) income.

Name	Age	Annual Income (thousand US$)
B	38	100
C	32	50
D	58	20

We can express the idea of "young," "old," and "several thousand dollars of income" using the fuzzy sets as shown in Figure 2.36.

Because A specifies "neither young nor old," we have to define a corresponding fuzzy set for the idea. Figure 2.37 shows the process of generating the fuzzy set for "neither young nor old."

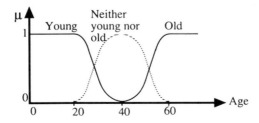

FIGURE 2.37. Fuzzy Sets for "young" and "old."

If we assign Y for a fuzzy set of "young" and O for a fuzzy set of "old," we will get

"not young" $\overline{Y}$

and

"not old" $\overline{O}$.

The fuzzy set "neither young nor old" can be generated by $\overline{Y} \cap \overline{O}$. This is because we can interpret the expression "neither young nor old" as the intersection of "not young" and "not old." If we write this idea by membership functions we get

$$\mu_{\overline{Y} \cap \overline{O}}(x) = \left(1 - \mu_Y(x)\right) \wedge \left(1 - \mu_O(x)\right).$$

Comparing the previously obtained fuzzy set "neither young nor old" and the actual age of each candidate, we can obtain the membership value of the individual age for the criterion. If we apply the same procedure to the income level, we will get the membership value of the candidates for A's ideal as follows.

Name	Age	Income	Total
B	0.9	1.0	0.9
C	0.6	0.5	0.5
D	0.2	0	0

These total evaluation scores are obtained by the min-operation of membership values for age and income. This implies if either age and income is far from the ideal, the candidate becomes unqualified. The value of the total evaluation may be interpreted as showing the degree of matching. If A gives a minimum satisfaction level of 0.8 for the total score, B will be introduced to A.

There will be various other methods to determine the total score. The multiplication of age and income membership values or the average of the two can be used.

2.5.2 Business Itinerary

When a teacher in Kanazawa goes to Tokyo, the itinerary can be evaluated by L-R fuzzy numbers.

Let the following be four methods of transportation and consider which will best suit his itinerary. The following are the one-way costs and the times of travel.

Method	Transportation	Cost (US$)	Time (hours)	Remarks
1	bullet train	240	4	
2	express train	190	6	
3	airplane	280	2	includes transit to airport
4	car	270	6–8	includes gas and highway toll

The evaluation of transportation method is defined as

(evaluation) = (time [hour]) + (cost [US $100]).

The preceding evaluation weights time at US$100 and the smaller the value, the better the evaluation.

The time for each method of transportation does not include delays, time required for transfer, and so on. If we include such factors, L-R fuzzy numbers to represent the time can be expressed as follows.

Method 1 $M_1 = (4.5, 0.5, 0.5)_{LR}$;

Method 2 $M_2 = (6.5, 0.5, 0.5)_{LR}$

Method 3 $M_3 = (2.5, 0.5, 1.0)_{LR}$

Method 4 $M_4 = (7.5, 1.0, 3.0)_{LR}$.

Figure 2.38 shows these L-R fuzzy numbers. L-R fuzzy numbers for the airplane and car have wider ranges of values compared with those of trains. The time may vary for a car depending on the road traffic conditions and airplanes tend to be late compared to trains.

Here, $L(x)$ and $R(x)$ are such that

$$L(x) = \max(0, 1 - |x|)$$
$$R(x) = \max(0, 1 - |x|).$$

On the other hand, L-R fuzzy numbers for the costs will be

Method 1 $N_1 = (2.4, 10^{-5}, 10^{-5})_{LR}$

Method 2 $N_2 = (1.9, 10^{-5}, 10^{-5})_{LR}$

Method 3 $N_3 = (2.8, 10^{-5}, 10^{-5})_{LR}$

Method 4 $N_4 = (2.7, 10^{-5}, 10^{-5})_{LR}$.

Although the costs are definite values, they are assumed as L-R fuzzy numbers with zero range. However, from the definition of L-R fuzzy numbers, $\alpha, \beta > 0$. Therefore I use a very small value 10^{-5} as an alternative.

The evaluation, from the costs and times, can be defined as follows.

(fuzzy number of evaluation) = (fuzzy number for time)

$\oplus$ (fuzzy number for costs).

The fuzzy numbers calculated as in the preceding will be

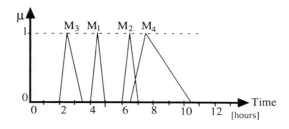

FIGURE 2.38. L-R fuzzy numbers for time.

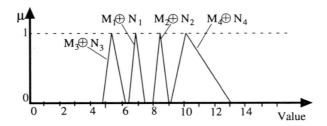

FIGURE 2.39. L-R fuzzy numbers for evaluation.

Method 1 $M_1 \oplus N_1 = (6.9, 0.5, 0.5)_{LR}$

Method 2 $M_2 \oplus N_2 = (8.5, 0.5, 0.5)_{LR}$

Method 3 $M_3 \oplus N_3 = (5.3, 0.5, 1.0)_{LR}$

Method 4 $M_4 \oplus N_4 = (10.2, 0.5, 3.0)_{LR}$.

These fuzzy numbers are shown in Figure 2.39, which tells us Method 3 is a good (low evaluation value) method.

Next, let us suppose a situation when the Kanazawa area was hit by a heavy snowfall. In such a case the fuzzy numbers for time will change as follows.

Method 1 $M_1^* = (5.0, 0.5, 1.0)_{LR}$

Method 2 $M_2^* = (7.0, 0.5, 1.0)_{LR}$

Method 3 $M_3^* = (5.0, 0.5, 3.0)_{LR}$

Method 4 $M_4^* = (12.0, 2.0, 5.0)_{LR}$.

These L-R fuzzy numbers are shown in Figure 2.40. The figure indicates that in case of heavy snow, uncertainty toward time delay will generally increase and it is particularly so for airplanes and cars. The evaluation of transportation will then be

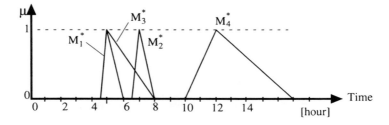

FIGURE 2.40. L-R Fuzzy numbers for time in case of heavy snow.

Method 1 $M_1^* \oplus N_1 = (7.4, 0.5, 1.0)_{LR}$

Method 2 $M_2^* \oplus N_2 = (9.0, 0.5, 1.0)_{LR}$

Method 3 $M_3^* \oplus N_3 = (7.8, 0.5, 3.0)_{LR}$

Method 4 $M_4^* \oplus N_4 = (14.7, 2.0, 5.0)_{LR}$.

Figure 2.41 shows these L-R fuzzy numbers, and from the figure we conclude Method 1 is good when heavy snow falls.

Next, let us think of the same method of transportation for a group of four people. For simplicity assume they are all adults. In such a case, all the costs except for the car are quadruple. Therefore the L-R fuzzy numbers for costs will now be:

Method 1 $N_1^* = (9.6, 10^{-5}, 10^{-5})_{LR}$

Method 2 $N_2^* = (8.0, 10^{-5}, 10^{-5})_{LR}$

Method 3 $N_3^* = (11.2, 10^{-5}, 10^{-5})_{LR}$

Method 4 $N_4^* = (2.7, 10^{-5}, 10^{-5})_{LR}$.

If time fuzzy numbers are as shown in Figure 2.38, the evaluation will change such as:

Method 1 $M_1 \oplus N_1^* = (14.1, 0.5, 0.5)_{LR}$

Method 2 $M_2 \oplus N_2^* = (14.5, 0.5, 0.5)_{LR}$

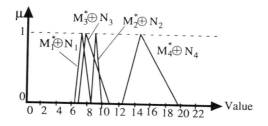

FIGURE 2.41. L-R fuzzy numbers for evaluation in case of heavy snow.

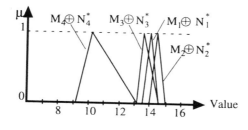

FIGURE 2.42. L-R fuzzy numbers for group travel.

Method 3 $M_3 \oplus N_3^* = (13.7, 0.5, 1.0)_{LR}$

Method 4 $M_4 \oplus N_4^* = (10.2, 1.0, 3.0)_{LR}$.

These fuzzy sets are shown in Figure 2.42. From the preceding fuzzy numbers, for group travel by four people, transportation by car is definitely good.

References

[1] Zadeh, L. A. 1965. Fuzzy sets. *Information and Control* 8; 338–353.
[2] Dubois, D. and Prade, H. 1980. *Fuzzy Sets and Systems Theory and Applications*. Academic Press, New York.

3

Fuzzy Relations

This chapter describes fuzzy relations. Fuzzy relation is an extension of relations in conventional set theory. Conventional relations are given by sets, and fuzzy relations are given by fuzzy sets. First, the definitions and properties are given, and operations of fuzzy relations are described. Then, composition of the fuzzy relation, an important concept for application, is presented.

3.1 Fuzzy Relations

Before describing the definition of fuzzy relation, I give two examples of fuzzy relations.

One example is an extension of crisp relations. Figure 3.1 compares a crisp relation and a fuzzy relation. The difference between the two is the same as that of crisp sets and fuzzy sets—whether they are defined by an exact boundary or not.

Another example of fuzzy relations is that a fuzzy relation is a fuzzy set on a multidimensional space (such as a Cartesian product space). A fuzzy set is given, as shown in Figure 3.2(a), on one universe (in the figure's case, the horizontal axis **X**). For example, the fuzzy set of "medium height" is expressed on the horizontal axis of height, and the fuzzy set of "middle age" is expressed on the horizontal axis of age. On the other hand, the fuzzy relation between height and age is expressed on

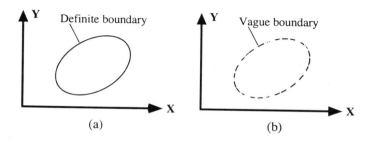

FIGURE 3.1. Image of fuzzy relations (1): (a) crisp relation; (b) fuzzy relation.

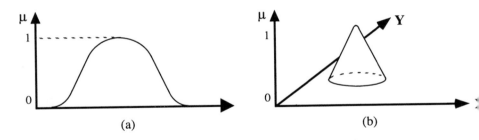

FIGURE 3.2. Image of fuzzy relations (2): (a) fuzzy set; (b) fuzzy relation.

the multidimensional space of height and age, as shown in Figure 3.2(b). Because the multidimensional space is given by the Cartesian product of related sets as shown in Section 2.4.1, a fuzzy relation is a fuzzy set on a Cartesian product space.

3.1.1 n-ary Fuzzy Relations

When we discuss fuzzy relation in general, we use the idea of n-ary fuzzy relations. In practice, n is replaced with a specific integer of 2 or larger, such as binary fuzzy relations for two-dimensional cases. The binary fuzzy relation defines the relations between two variables. In the following text, I first describe a general expression of n-ary fuzzy relation, and then binary fuzzy relation, which is the most fundamental of fuzzy relations.

n-ary fuzzy relation

An n-ary fuzzy relation R is defined on the Cartesian product of $X_1 \times \cdots \times X_n$ of sets $X_1, \ldots, X_n$ such as:

$$R = \int_{X_1 \times \cdots \times X_n} \mu_R(x_1, x_2, \ldots, x_n)/(x_1, x_2, \ldots, x_n), \qquad (3.1)$$

where μ_R is the membership function of R given as

$$\mu_R : X_1 \times \cdots \times X_n \rightarrow [0, 1]. \qquad (3.2)$$

As I explained in the second image of fuzzy relations, the membership function μ_R represents a fuzzy set on the multidimensional space $X_1 \times \cdots \times X_n$. In crisp relations (3.2) is replaced with

$$\mu_R(x_1, x_2, \ldots, x_n) = \begin{cases} 1 & (x_1, , x_2, \ldots, x_n) \in R, \\ 0 & \text{(otherwise)}. \end{cases} \qquad (3.3)$$

The preceding equation is an extension of the characteristic function of crisp sets defined by (2.11).

EXAMPLE 3.1. FUZZY RELATIONS AND CRISP RELATIONS

Relations such as "y equals x" and "y is smaller than x" are crisp relations. Figure 3.3(a) and (b) shows these two crisp relations. In both cases, boundaries are explicitly defined.

On the other hand, we cannot define the boundaries in such cases as "y is about the same as x" and "y is slightly smaller than x" and these relations are fuzzy relations. Fuzzy relations express the degree of being "about the same" and "slightly smaller" in arbitrary real values between 0 and 1.

The fuzzy relations shown in the preceding example indicate the relations between two variables, x and y. Therefore these relations are binary relations. Hereafter the discussions are focused on the binary relations.

Binary fuzzy relation (continuous expression)

The binary fuzzy relation R between sets X and Y are defined as

$$R = \int_{X \times Y} \mu_R(x, y)/(x, y), \tag{3.4}$$

where μ_R is the membership function of R given by the Cartesian product X × Y as

$$\mu_R : X \times Y \to [0, 1]. \tag{3.5}$$

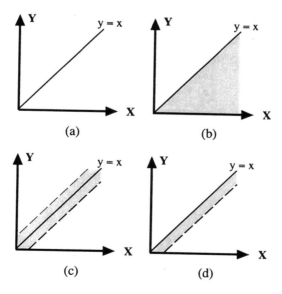

FIGURE 3.3. Crisp relations (a) "y equals x," and (b) "y is smaller than x." Fuzzy relations (c) "y is about the same as x," and "y is slightly smaller than x."

We can get the preceding definition by substituting $n = 2, X_1 = Y,$ and $X_2 = Y$ in (3.1). When $X = Y$, we specifically call R "a fuzzy relation on X."

The definition of binary fuzzy relation (3.4) is given in a continuous expression. We can write this relation by a discrete expression.

Binary fuzzy relation (discrete expression)

Let the universe X and Y be given as

$$X = \{x_1, x_2, \ldots, x_n\}$$
$$Y = \{y_1, y_2, \ldots, y_m\}.$$

The binary fuzzy relation of X and Y is expressed in the matrix expression:

$$R = \begin{array}{c} \\ x_1 \\ x_2 \\ \vdots \\ x_n \end{array} \begin{array}{ccccc} y_1 & y_2 & \cdots & y_{m-1} & y_m \\ \left[\begin{array}{ccccc} \mu_R(x_1, y_1) & \mu_R(x_1, y_2) & \cdots & \mu_R(x_1, y_{m-1}) & \mu_R(x_1, y_m) \\ \mu_R(x_2, y_1) & \mu_R(x_2, y_2) & \cdots & \mu_R(x_2, y_{m-1}) & \mu_R(x_2, y_m) \\ \vdots & \vdots & \ddots & \vdots & \vdots \\ \mu_R(x_n, y_1) & \mu_R(x_n, y_2) & \cdots & \mu_R(x_n, y_{m-1}) & \mu_R(x_n, y_m) \end{array}\right] \end{array}$$

$$(3.6)$$

A matrix expressing a fuzzy relation is sometimes called a fuzzy matrix.

EXAMPLE 3.2. AN EXAMPLE OF FUZZY RELATIONS

Let us choose three cities x_1, x_2, and x_3 in New York State and three more y_1, y_2, and y_3 from adjacent New Jersey. Considering these cities as elements of respective sets X and Y, we can write

$$X = \{x_1, x_2, x_3\}$$
$$Y = \{y_1, y_2, y_3\}.$$

Assume we can define a fuzzy relation of "close" that can be expressed as

$$\text{"close"} = \begin{array}{c} \\ x_1 \\ x_2 \\ x_3 \end{array} \begin{array}{ccc} y_1 & y_2 & y_3 \\ \left[\begin{array}{ccc} 1 & 0.6 & 0.3 \\ 0.4 & 0.9 & 0.1 \\ 0.5 & 0.2 & 0.7 \end{array}\right] \end{array}.$$

In this fuzzy relation, "close," the degree of closeness between x_1 and y_2 is 0.6 and the degree of closeness between x_1 and y_1 is 1.0. This means that y_1 is closer to x_1 than y_2. The value of each element should be determined appropriately as in the case of membership functions for fuzzy sets.

If we define the "close" meaning as less than 100 km, the relation of the cities is reduced into a crisp relation that takes either 0 or 1 for the value of the elements such as

$$\text{"close"} = \begin{array}{c} \\ x_1 \\ x_2 \\ x_3 \end{array} \begin{array}{ccc} y_1 & y_2 & y_3 \\ \left[\begin{array}{ccc} 1 & 1 & 0 \\ 0 & 1 & 0 \\ 0 & 0 & 1 \end{array} \right] \end{array}.$$

Such a matrix is called a Boolean matrix in contrast to a fuzzy matrix.

Also, we sometimes express a fuzzy relation "R" representing the relation of universe X and Y such as

$$R \subset X \times Y.$$

EXAMPLE 3.3. MARITAL RELATIONS AND INTIMATE RELATIONS

I have shown that fuzzy relations can deal with relations defined in a vague phrase such as "y is slightly smaller than x." The real-world relations are all fuzzy relations. A typical example is personal relations. In this example, I show relations of men and women as an example of fuzzy relation.

Suppose there are three fictitious couples Karen and David, Joan and Michael, and Helen and Gary. If all those couples are married, their marital relations can be expressed by a Boolean matrix such as

$$\text{"married"} = \begin{array}{c} \\ \text{David} \\ \text{Michael} \\ \text{Gary} \end{array} \begin{array}{ccc} \text{Karen} & \text{Joan} & \text{Helen} \\ \left[\begin{array}{ccc} 1 & 0 & 0 \\ 0 & 1 & 0 \\ 0 & 0 & 1 \end{array} \right] \end{array}.$$

However, gossip says their intimate relations are somewhat different. Let us assume that the intimacy between a man and a woman can be measured in the value between 0 and 1. Then, the degree of intimacy caused by gossip can be expressed by a fuzzy relation such as

$$\text{"intimate"} = \begin{array}{c} \\ \text{David} \\ \text{Michael} \\ \text{Gary} \end{array} \begin{array}{ccc} \text{Karen} & \text{Joan} & \text{Helen} \\ \left[\begin{array}{ccc} 1.0 & 0 & 0.2 \\ 0.1 & 0.3 & 1.0 \\ 0.3 & 0.9 & 0.5 \end{array} \right] \end{array}.$$

I leave it to the readers' imaginations as to how their illicit relations develop but one clear point is that by fuzzy relations we can express such a vague relation as "intimate" as far as we can define the degree of intimacy.

To represent fuzzy relations by computer we can remember how we dealt with fuzzy sets. Fuzzy sets are represented by one-dimensional arrays on computers. The binary fuzzy relation (fuzzy matrix) in the preceding example can be then represented by a two-dimensional array as in Figure 3.4. In general, n-ary fuzzy relations can be stored in n-dimensional arrays.

	y_1	y_2	y_3
x_1	1.0	0.0	0.2
x_2	0.1	0.3	1.0
x_3	0.3	0.9	0.5

FIGURE 3.4. Representation of fuzzy relations by computers.

3.1.2 Projection of Fuzzy Relations and Cylindrical Extension

In this section I describe the projection of fuzzy relations and cylindrical extension. First, the definition of projection of n-ary fuzzy relations and cylindrical extension is given. Then, a simplified definition is shown for binary fuzzy relations.

Projection and cylindrical extension (n-ary fuzzy relation)

- Projection of fuzzy relations: let R be a fuzzy relation on the Cartesian product $X_1 \times \cdots \times X_n$, and array $(i_1, \ldots, i_k)$ be a subarray of $(1, \ldots, n)$. The projection of R on $X_{i_1}, \ldots, X_{i_k}$ is defined as

$$\text{proj}[R; X_{i_1}, \ldots, X_{i_k}]$$

$$= \int_{X_{i_1} \times \cdots \times X_{i_k}} \max_{X_{j_1} \times \cdots \times X_{j_m}} \mu_R(x_1, \ldots, x_n)/(x_{i_1}, \ldots, x_{i_k}), \qquad (3.7)$$

where the array $(j_1, \ldots, j_m)$ is the complementary of $(i_1, \ldots, i_k)$, that is, the subarray of $(1, \ldots, n)$ with $(i_1, \ldots, i_k)$ subtracted.

- Cylindrical extension: let R be a fuzzy relation on the Cartesian product of $X_1 \times \cdots \times X_n$. The cylindrical extension $c(R)$ of R on $X_1 \times \cdots \times X_n$ is defined as

$$c(R) = \int_{X_1 \times \cdots \times X_n} \mu_R(x_1, x_2, \ldots, x_n)/(x_1, x_2, \ldots, x_n). \qquad (3.8)$$

Equations (3.7) and (3.8) are the general definition of projection and cylindrical extension in an n-ary case. Next, I give the definitions in a binary case to facilitate the readers' understanding.

Projection and cylindrical extension (binary fuzzy relation in continuous expression)

- Projection of fuzzy relations: let R be a fuzzy relation on a Cartesian product X × Y. The projection of R on X is a fuzzy set defined as

$$\text{proj}[R; X] = \int_X \left(\max_y \mu_R(x, y) \right) / x. \tag{3.9}$$

The projection of R on Y is also a fuzzy set and can be defined as

$$\text{proj}[R; Y] = \int_Y \left(\max_x \mu_R(x, y) \right) / y. \tag{3.10}$$

- Cylindrical extension: let A be a fuzzy set on the universe X. The cylindrical extension c(A) of A on X × Y can be defined by the fuzzy relation

$$c(A) = \int_{X \times Y} \mu_A(x)/(x, y). \tag{3.11}$$

Let B be a fuzzy set on the universe Y. The cylindrical extension c(B) of B on X × Y can be defined by the fuzzy relation

$$c(B) = \int_{X \times Y} \mu_B(y)/(x, y). \tag{3.12}$$

Equations (3.9)–(3.12) are given in continuous expressions. If we rewrite these equations with discrete equations they will be as follows.

Projection and cylindrical extension (Binary fuzzy relation in discrete expression)

Suppose the universe X and Y are given such as:

X = {x_1, x_2, ..., x_n}
Y = {y_1, y_2, ..., y_m}.

- Projection of fuzzy relations: let R be a fuzzy relation on a Cartesian product X × Y. The projection of R on X is a fuzzy set defined as

$$\text{proj}[R; X] = \sum_{i=1}^{n} \left\{ \max_{y_j \in Y} \mu_R(x_i, y_j) \right\} / x)i. \tag{3.13}$$

The projection of R on Y is also a fuzzy set and can be defined as

$$\text{proj}[R; Y] = \sum_{j=1}^{n} \left\{ \max_{x_i \in X} \mu_R(x_i, y_j) \right\} / y_i. \tag{3.14}$$

- Cylindrical extension: let A be a fuzzy set on the universe X. The cylindrical extension c(A) of A on X × Y can be defined by the fuzzy matrix

$$c(A) = \begin{array}{c} \\ x_1 \\ x_2 \\ \vdots \\ x_n \end{array} \begin{array}{cccc} y_1 & y_2 & \cdots & y_{m-1} & y_m \\ \left[\begin{array}{ccccc} \mu_A(x_1) & \mu_A(x_1) & \cdots & \mu_A(x_1) & \mu_A(x_1) \\ \mu_A(x_2) & \mu_A(x_2) & \cdots & \mu_A(x_2) & \mu_A(x_2) \\ \vdots & \vdots & \ddots & \vdots & \vdots \\ \mu_A(x_n) & \mu_A(x_n) & \cdots & \mu_A(x_n) & \mu_A(x_n) \end{array}\right] \end{array} \quad (3.15)$$

Let B be a fuzzy set on the universe Y. The cylindrical extension c(B) of B on X × Y can be defined by the fuzzy matrix

$$c(B) = \begin{array}{c} \\ x_1 \\ x_2 \\ \vdots \\ x_n \end{array} \begin{array}{ccccc} y_1 & y_2 & \cdots & y_{m-1} & y_m \\ \left[\begin{array}{ccccc} \mu_B(y_1) & \mu_B(y_2) & \cdots & \mu_B(y_{m-1}) & \mu_B(y_m) \\ \mu_B(y_1) & \mu_B(y_2) & \cdots & \mu_B(y_{m-1}) & \mu_B(y_m) \\ \vdots & \vdots & \vdots & \ddots & \vdots & \vdots \\ \mu_B(y_1) & \mu_B(y_2) & \cdots & \mu_B(y_{m-1}) & \mu_B(y_m) \end{array}\right] \end{array}$$

$$(3.16)$$

Figures 3.5 and 3.6 show the ideas of projection and cylindrical extension. Obviously, projection and cylindrical extension are opposite operations.

EXAMPLE 3.4. PROJECTION AND CYLINDRICAL EXTENSION

Suppose the universe X and Y are given as

$$X = \{x_1, x_2, x_3\}$$
$$Y = \{y_1, y_2, y_3\}.$$

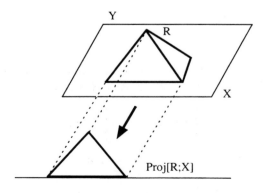

FIGURE 3.5. Projection.

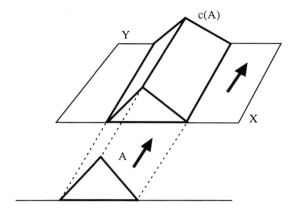

FIGURE 3.6. Cylindrical extension.

Now let us consider a fuzzy relation R on $X \times Y$ such as:

$$R = \begin{array}{c} \\ x_1 \\ x_2 \\ x_3 \end{array} \begin{array}{ccc} y_1 & y_2 & y_3 \\ \left[\begin{array}{ccc} 0.6 & 1 & 0.3 \\ 0.5 & 0.2 & 0.8 \\ 0.1 & 0.4 & 0.7 \end{array} \right] \end{array}.$$

The projection of R on X is then calculated as

$$\begin{aligned} \text{proj}[R; X] &= \max(0.6, 1, 0.3)/x_1 \\ &\quad + \max(0.5, 0.2, 0.8)/x_2 \\ &\quad + \max(0.1, 0.4, 0.7)/x_3 \\ &= 1/x_1 + 0.8/x_2 + 0.7/x_3 = A. \end{aligned}$$

Here A is the fuzzy set projected on X.

On the other hand, the projection of R on Y is calculated as

$$\begin{aligned} \text{proj}[R; Y] &= \max(0.6, 0.5, 0.1)/y_1 \\ &\quad + \max(1, 0.2, 0.4)/y_2 \\ &\quad + \max(0.3, 0.8, 0.7)/y_3 \\ &= 0.6/y_1 + 1/y_2 + 0.8/y_3 = B. \end{aligned}$$

The cylindrical extension of the fuzzy set A on the Cartesian product $X \times Y$ is then

$$c(A) = \begin{array}{c} \\ x_1 \\ x_2 \\ x_3 \end{array} \begin{array}{ccc} y_1 & y_2 & y_3 \\ \left[\begin{array}{ccc} 1 & 1 & 1 \\ 0.8 & 0.8 & 0.8 \\ 0.7 & 0.7 & 0.7 \end{array} \right] \end{array}.$$

Also, the cylindrical extension of B on X × Y is

$$
c(B) = \begin{array}{c} \\ x_1 \\ x_2 \\ x_3 \end{array}
\begin{array}{ccc} y_1 & y_2 & y_3 \\ \left[\begin{array}{ccc} 0.6 & 1 & 0.8 \\ 0.6 & 1 & 0.8 \\ 0.6 & 1 & 0.8 \end{array}\right]. \end{array}
$$

Now let us think of the meaning of projections by (3.13) and (3.14). Figure 3.7 shows the idea of projection. Assume the values of matrix elements (membership value) show the height of objects. By illuminating the objects in the direction shown in Figure 3.7, we will get shadows on a wall on the Y-axis. This operation represents the projection on the Y-axis, and the shadows portray the fuzzy sets obtained by the projection. Naturally, the shadows reflect the height of the highest objects in a column. This equals the max-operation in (3.13) and (3.14). For example, at the position of y_1, the maximum of (0.1, 0.5, 0.6), that is, 0.6 is projected as the shadow.

EXAMPLE 3.5. INTERSECTION OF " MODERATE HEIGHT" AND " MIDDLE AGE"

The main point of this example is how we can obtain the intersection of a fuzzy set representing "moderate height" and another fuzzy set for "middle age." Can we express the intersection of "moderate height" and "middle age" as

"Moderate height" ∩ "Middle age"?

If the operation of the preceding intersection could be defined, it would be something like that shown in Figure 3.8. However, because the horizontal axes are different for the height and the age, we cannot formally derive such an operation. Then how can we obtain the intersection of "moderate height" and "middle age?" I show the appropriate procedure in the following text.

When we have fuzzy sets on different universes, such as "moderate height" and "middle age," we can apply an operation depicted in Figure 3.9. Note that we have the universes of *height* and *age* and we need to think of their intersection in the Cartesian space of *height* × *age*. Because the fuzzy set "moderate height" is not related to age, we make a cylindrical extension of "moderate height" towards

FIGURE 3.7. An idea of projection.

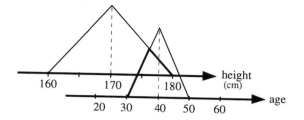

FIGURE 3.8. Intersection of "moderate height" and "middle-age"

height × *age* space. Let us denote this extension as

c(moderate height) = *moderate height* × *age.*

Similarly, we make a cylindrical extension of "middle age" towards *age* × *height* space and obtain

c(middle age) = *middle age* × *height.*

Both these cylindrical extensions are fuzzy sets on *height* × *age* and now we can take the intersection of these two. Therefore we obtain the operation of (*moderate height* × *age*) ∩ (*middle age* × *height*). The details of the intersection of fuzzy relations are described in Section 3.2.

3.1.3 Converse Fuzzy Relations and Other Relations

In this section I introduce special fuzzy relations such as the converse fuzzy relation.

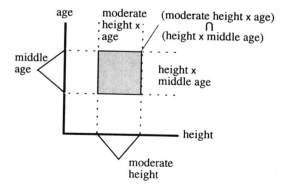

FIGURE 3.9. Intersection of fuzzy relations.

Converse fuzzy relations and other relations

Here we consider binary fuzzy relations on X × Y.

- Converse fuzzy relation: (R^{-1}): the converse fuzzy relation of fuzzy relation R is a fuzzy relation defined by the membership function

$$\mu_{R^{-1}}(y, x) = \mu_R(x, y). \tag{3.17}$$

- Identity relation I: identity relation I is defined by the membership function

$$\mu_I(x, y) = \begin{cases} 1 & x = y \\ 0 & x \neq y \end{cases}. \tag{3.18}$$

- Zero relation Z: zero relation Z can be defined by the membership function as

$$\mu_Z(x, y) = 0 \quad \forall x \in x, \quad \forall y \in Y. \tag{3.19}$$

- Universe relation: universe relation U can be defined by the membership function as

$$\mu_U(x, y) = 1 \quad \forall_x \in X, \quad \forall_y \in Y. \tag{3.20}$$

EXAMPLE 3.6. CONVERSE FUZZY RELATIONS, IDENTITY RELATION, ZERO RELATION, AND UNIVERSE RELATION

Suppose a fuzzy relation R is given by

$$R = \begin{bmatrix} 1.0 & 0.8 & 0.4 \\ 0.7 & 0.3 & 0.6 \\ 0.1 & 0.5 & 0.9 \end{bmatrix}.$$

The converse fuzzy relation is

$$R^{-1} = \begin{bmatrix} 1.0 & 0.7 & 0.1 \\ 0.8 & 0.3 & 0.5 \\ 0.4 & 0.6 & 0.9 \end{bmatrix}.$$

Identity relation I, zero relation Z, and universe relation U are given in a matrix form as

$$I = \begin{bmatrix} 1 & 0 & 0 \\ 0 & 1 & 0 \\ 0 & 0 & 1 \end{bmatrix} \quad Z = \begin{bmatrix} 0 & 0 & 0 \\ 0 & 0 & 0 \\ 0 & 0 & 0 \end{bmatrix} \quad U = \begin{bmatrix} 1 & 1 & 1 \\ 1 & 1 & 1 \\ 1 & 1 & 1 \end{bmatrix}.$$

3.2 Operations of Fuzzy Relations

Operations of fuzzy sets are defined, as are similar operations of fuzzy relations. Because fuzzy relations are expressed by fuzzy sets on a Cartesian product space, we can apply the same operations as fuzzy sets on fuzzy relations. I first give the union, intersection, and complement of fuzzy relations.

Union, intersection, and complement of fuzzy relations

Let R, S be fuzzy relations on X × Y. The union, intersection, and complement are defined by the respective membership functions as follows.

- Union of fuzzy relations: R ∪ S

$$\mu_{R \cup S}(x, y) = \mu_R(x, y) \vee \mu_S(x, y).$$ (3.21)

- Intersection of fuzzy relations: R ∩ S

$$\mu_{R \cap S}(x, y) = \mu_R(x, y) \wedge \mu_S(x, y).$$ (3.22)

- Complement of fuzzy relation:

$$\mu_{\bar{R}}(x, y) = 1 - \mu_R(x, y).$$ (3.23)

Next let us consider the definition of inclusion of fuzzy sets. Because fuzzy relations are fuzzy sets on Cartesian product space, the inclusion of fuzzy relations is defined by fuzzy sets.

Inclusion of fuzzy relations

Let R, S be fuzzy relations on X × Y. The inclusion of fuzzy relations R and S is defined by the membership function:

$$R \subseteq S \Leftrightarrow \mu_R(x, y) \leq \mu_S(x, y), \quad \forall x \in X \quad \forall y \in Y.$$ (3.24)

Although I have shown the complement of fuzzy relation $\bar{R}$ in (3.23), note that the converse fuzzy relation R^{-1} is different from $\bar{R}$.

The properties of converse fuzzy relations are listed as follows.

Properties of converse fuzzy relations

i. $(R \cup S)^{-1} = R^{-1} \cup S^{-1}$.

ii. $(R \cap S)^{-1} = R^{-1} \cap S^{-1}$.

iii. $\left(R^{-1}\right)^{-1} = R$. (3.25)

iv. $\overline{\left(R^{-1}\right)} = \left(\bar{R}\right)^{-1}$.

v. $R \subseteq S = R^{-1} \subseteq S^{-1}$.

EXAMPLE 3.7. PROPERTIES OF CONVERSE FUZZY RELATIONS

In this example, let us prove the five properties of converse fuzzy relations shown by (3.25). Suppose the following fuzzy relations R and S are given as

$$
R = \begin{array}{c} \\ x_1 \\ x_2 \\ x_3 \end{array}
\begin{array}{ccc} y_1 & y_2 & y_3 \\ \left[\begin{array}{ccc} 1.0 & 0.8 & 0.4 \\ 0.7 & 0.3 & 0.6 \\ 0.1 & 0.5 & 0.9 \end{array}\right] \end{array}
\qquad
S = \begin{array}{c} \\ x_1 \\ x_2 \\ x_3 \end{array}
\begin{array}{ccc} y_1 & y_2 & y_3 \\ \left[\begin{array}{ccc} 0.2 & 0.1 & 0.6 \\ 0.9 & 0.8 & 0.5 \\ 0.3 & 0.2 & 1.0 \end{array}\right] \end{array}.
$$

i. $(R \cup S)^{-1} = R^{-1} \cup S^{-1}$. $R \cup S$ is

$$
R \cup S = \begin{bmatrix} 1.0 & 0.8 & 0.6 \\ 0.9 & 0.8 & 0.6 \\ 0.3 & 0.5 & 1.0 \end{bmatrix}.
$$

Then the converse fuzzy relation $(R \cup S)^{-1}$ is

$$
(R \cup S)^{-1} = \begin{bmatrix} 1.0 & 0.9 & 0.3 \\ 0.8 & 0.8 & 0.5 \\ 0.6 & 0.6 & 1.0 \end{bmatrix}.
$$

On the other hand, the converse fuzzy relations for R and S are, respectively,

$$
R^{-1} = \begin{bmatrix} 1.0 & 0.7 & 0.1 \\ 0.8 & 0.3 & 0.5 \\ 0.4 & 0.6 & 0.9 \end{bmatrix}
\qquad
S^{-1} = \begin{bmatrix} 0.2 & 0.9 & 0.3 \\ 0.1 & 0.8 & 0.2 \\ 0.6 & 0.5 & 1.0 \end{bmatrix}.
$$

Therefore $R^{-1} \cup S^{-1}$ is

$$
R^{-1} \cup S^{-1} = \begin{bmatrix} 1.0 & 0.9 & 0.3 \\ 0.8 & 0.8 & 0.5 \\ 0.6 & 0.6 & 1.0 \end{bmatrix}.
$$

Thus $(R \cup S)^{-1} = R^{-1} \cup S^{-1}$.

ii. $(R \cap S)^{-1} = R^{-1} \cap S^{-1}$. $R \cap S$ is

$$
R \cap S = \begin{bmatrix} 0.2 & 0.1 & 0.4 \\ 0.7 & 0.3 & 0.5 \\ 0.1 & 0.2 & 0.9 \end{bmatrix}.
$$

The converse fuzzy relation is

$$
(R \cap S)^{-1} = \begin{bmatrix} 0.2 & 0.7 & 0.1 \\ 0.1 & 0.3 & 0.2 \\ 0.4 & 0.5 & 0.9 \end{bmatrix}.
$$

On the other hand, the converse fuzzy relations for R and S are, respectively,

$$
R^{-1} = \begin{bmatrix} 1.0 & 0.7 & 0.1 \\ 0.8 & 0.3 & 0.5 \\ 0.4 & 0.6 & 0.9 \end{bmatrix}
\qquad
S^{-1} = \begin{bmatrix} 0.2 & 0.9 & 0.3 \\ 0.1 & 0.8 & 0.2 \\ 0.6 & 0.5 & 1.0 \end{bmatrix}.
$$

Therefore $R^{-1} \cap S^{-1}$ is

$$R^{-1} \cap S^{-1} = \begin{bmatrix} 0.2 & 0.7 & 0.1 \\ 0.1 & 0.3 & 0.2 \\ 0.4 & 0.5 & 0.9 \end{bmatrix}.$$

Thus $(R \cap S)^{-1} = R^{-1} \cap S^{-1}$.

iii. $(R^{-1})^{-1} = R$. Converse fuzzy relations are given by the transposed fuzzy matrix. It is obvious that $(R^{-1})^{-1} = R$ because

$$(R^{-1})^{-1} = \begin{bmatrix} 1.0 & 0.7 & 0.1 \\ 0.8 & 0.3 & 0.5 \\ 0.4 & 0.6 & 0.9 \end{bmatrix}^T = \begin{bmatrix} 1.0 & 0.8 & 0.4 \\ 0.7 & 0.3 & 0.6 \\ 0.1 & 0.5 & 0.9 \end{bmatrix} = R.$$

iv. $\overline{(R^{-1})} = (\overline{R})^{-1}$. The converse fuzzy relation of R is

$$R^{-1} = \begin{bmatrix} 1.0 & 0.7 & 0.1 \\ 0.8 & 0.3 & 0.5 \\ 0.4 & 0.6 & 0.9 \end{bmatrix}.$$

The complement of R^{-1} is, therefore,

$$\overline{R^{-1}} = \begin{bmatrix} 0 & 0.3 & 0.9 \\ 0.2 & 0.7 & 0.5 \\ 0.6 & 0.4 & 0.1 \end{bmatrix}.$$

On the other hand, the complement of R is

$$\overline{R} = \begin{bmatrix} 0 & 0.2 & 0.6 \\ 0.3 & 0.7 & 0.4 \\ 0.9 & 0.5 & 0.1 \end{bmatrix}.$$

Therefore the converse fuzzy relation is

$$(\overline{R})^{-1} = \begin{bmatrix} 0 & 0.3 & 0.9 \\ 0.2 & 0.7 & 0.5 \\ 0.6 & 0.4 & 0.1 \end{bmatrix}.$$

Thus $\overline{(R^{-1})} = (\overline{R})^{-1}$.

v. $R \subseteq S = R^{-1} \subseteq S^{-1}$

$$S = \begin{bmatrix} 1.0 & 0.9 & 0.7 \\ 0.8 & 0.4 & 0.9 \\ 0.2 & 0.8 & 1.0 \end{bmatrix}$$

$$R^{-1} = \begin{bmatrix} 1.0 & 0.7 & 0.1 \\ 0.8 & 0.3 & 0.5 \\ 0.2 & 0.6 & 1.0 \end{bmatrix}$$

$$S^{-1} = \begin{bmatrix} 1.0 & 0.8 & 0.2 \\ 0.9 & 0.4 & 0.8 \\ 0.7 & 0.9 & 1.0 \end{bmatrix},$$

EXAMPLE 3.8. DE MORGAN'S LAWS

Suppose the universe X and Y are given as:

$X = \{x_1, x_2, x_3\}$

$Y = \{y_1, y_2, y_3\}$.

Let us consider a fuzzy relation R on $X \times Y$ such as:

$$R = \begin{array}{c} \\ x_1 \\ x_2 \\ x_3 \end{array} \begin{array}{ccc} y_1 & y_2 & y_3 \\ \begin{bmatrix} 1.0 & 0.4 & 0.6 \\ 0.5 & 0.8 & 0.7 \\ 0.9 & 0.6 & 1.0 \end{bmatrix} \end{array} \qquad S = \begin{array}{c} \\ x_1 \\ x_2 \\ x_3 \end{array} \begin{array}{ccc} y_1 & y_2 & y_3 \\ \begin{bmatrix} 0.3 & 0.7 & 0.9 \\ 0.6 & 1.0 & 0.4 \\ 0.2 & 0.9 & 1.0 \end{bmatrix} \end{array}.$$

Here $R \cup S$ and $R \cap S$ are

$$R \cup S = \begin{bmatrix} 1.0 & 0.7 & 0.9 \\ 0.6 & 1.0 & 0.7 \\ 0.9 & 0.9 & 1.0 \end{bmatrix} \qquad R \cap S = \begin{bmatrix} 0.3 & 0.4 & 0.6 \\ 0.5 & 0.8 & 0.4 \\ 0.2 & 0.6 & 1.0 \end{bmatrix}.$$

Therefore $\overline{R \cup S}$ and $\overline{R \cap S}$ are

$$\overline{R \cup S} = \begin{bmatrix} 0 & 0.3 & 0.1 \\ 0.4 & 0 & 0.3 \\ 0.1 & 0.1 & 0 \end{bmatrix} \qquad \overline{R \cap S} = \begin{bmatrix} 0.7 & 0.6 & 0.4 \\ 0.5 & 0.2 & 0.6 \\ 0.8 & 0.4 & 0 \end{bmatrix}.$$

On the other hand, $\overline{R}$ and $\overline{S}$ are

$$\overline{R} = \begin{bmatrix} 0 & 0.6 & 0.4 \\ 0.5 & 0.2 & 0.3 \\ 0.1 & 0.4 & 0 \end{bmatrix} \qquad \overline{S} = \begin{bmatrix} 0.7 & 0.3 & 0.1 \\ 0.4 & 0 & 0.6 \\ 0.8 & 0.1 & 0 \end{bmatrix}.$$

Then

$$\overline{R} \cup \overline{S} = \begin{bmatrix} 0.7 & 0.6 & 0.4 \\ 0.5 & 0.2 & 0.6 \\ 0.8 & 0.4 & 0 \end{bmatrix} = \overline{R \cap S}$$

and

$$\overline{R} \cap \overline{S} = \begin{bmatrix} 0 & 0.3 & 0.1 \\ 0.4 & 0 & 0.3 \\ 0.1 & 0.1 & 0 \end{bmatrix} = \overline{R \cup S}.$$

This proves De Morgan's law.

EXAMPLE 3.9. DOUBLE NEGATION LAW

If we refer to the definition of complement for a fuzzy relation given in (3.23), the double negation law is proved to be valid.
Consider a fuzzy relation given as

$$R = \begin{array}{c} \\ x_1 \\ x_2 \\ x_3 \end{array} \begin{array}{ccc} y_1 & y_2 & y_3 \\ \left[\begin{array}{ccc} 0.2 & 0.4 & 0.6 \\ 0.5 & 0.8 & 0.2 \\ 0.1 & 0.4 & 0.8 \end{array}\right] \end{array}.$$

The complement of R is

$$\overline{R} = \begin{bmatrix} 0.8 & 0.6 & 0.4 \\ 0.5 & 0.2 & 0.8 \\ 0.9 & 0.4 & 0.2 \end{bmatrix}.$$

If we further negate the preceding, we will get

$$\overline{\overline{R}} = \begin{bmatrix} 0.2 & 0.4 & 0.6 \\ 0.5 & 0.8 & 0.2 \\ 0.1 & 0.4 & 0.8 \end{bmatrix} = R.$$

In order to perform the operations of fuzzy relations on a computer, we should remember how we do the operations of fuzzy sets. Binary fuzzy relations are expressed by two-dimensional arrays and so involve their operations. For the intersection of fuzzy relations $R \cap S$, we compare the corresponding elements of the two-dimensional arrays R and S, and take the smaller value for the array of $R \cap S$. For the union of fuzzy relations $R \cup S$, on the other hand, we can take the larger value of the two corresponding elements to form $R \cup S$.
For example, if fuzzy relations R and H are given as

fuzzy relation R

1.0	0.8	0.4
0.7	0.8	0.5
0.1	0.5	0.9

fuzzy relation S

0.2	0.1	0.6
0.9	0.8	0.5
0.3	0.2	1.0

the intersection obtained is

fuzzy relation $R \cap S$

$1.0 \wedge 0.2 \rightarrow$

0.2	0.1	0.4
0.7	0.3	0.5
0.1	0.2	0.9

The shaded element is calculated from the definition as

$$1.0 \wedge 0.2 = 0.2.$$

If we perform the same operation for all the corresponding elements of R and S, we will get the preceding R ∩ S.

On the other hand, R ∪ S can be obtained as

fuzzy relation R∪S

$1.0 \vee 0.2 \rightarrow$

1.0	0.8	0.6
0.9	0.8	0.6
0.3	0.5	1.0

The shaded element is calculated from the definition such as

$$1.0 \vee 0.2 = 0.2.$$

If we perform the same operation for all the corresponding elements of R and S, we will get the preceding R ∪ S.

3.3 Composition of Fuzzy Relations

In this section I describe the composition of fuzzy relations. First, simple images of composition are shown, and then practical calculation procedure is described.

3.3.1 The Image of Composition

Before describing the details of calculating composition, I give its images. Figure 3.10 depicts the image of composition.

When there is a function $y = f(x)$, the value of y_0 for x_0 is given by

$$y_0 = f(x_0).$$

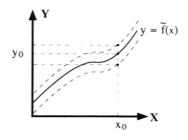

FIGURE 3.10. Image of composition (1).

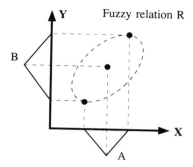

FIGURE 3.11. Image of composition (2).

Let us replace the function f with a vague function $\tilde{f}$, then. Here, $\sim$ means fuzzy expression. For this fuzzy function, we get the value of $\tilde{y}_0$ for x_0. Figure 3.10 shows such a calculation process. Because $\tilde{f}$ is a vague function, the value of y is not a definite value, but a vague value as $\tilde{y}_0$.

The function $\tilde{f}$ in Figure 3.10 is a special form of fuzzy relation. If we extend $\tilde{f}$ to a general fuzzy relation R, the image of composition will be such as shown in Figure 3.11. Suppose a binary fuzzy relation R on X × Y, and a fuzzy set A on X corresponds with another fuzzy set B on Y, then we can obtain the fuzzy set B such as

B = A ∘ R

where ∘ represents the composition.

As shown in Figure 3.12, if we consider A as the input, B as the output, and R as representing the input–output relation, B = A ∘ R can be regarded as representing the input–output relation equation. This idea corresponds with the fact that we can assume x_0 as input and y_0 as output, and f as the input–output relation.

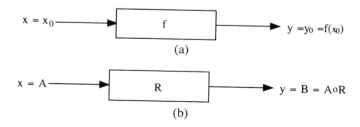

FIGURE 3.12. (a) Input-output relation of $y_0 = f(x_0)$; (b) input-output relation of B = A ∘ R.

3.3.2 Calculation of Composition

In this part of the section I describe a practical method for calculating the composition of fuzzy relations. There are two alternate ways of definitions as follows.

a. Composition A ∘ R defined with a fuzzy relation R on X × Y and a fuzzy set A on X.
b. Composition R ∘ S defined with a fuzzy relation R on X × Y and a fuzzy relation S on Y × Z.

If we consider the composition as an input-output relation such as shown in Section 3.3.1, the preceding definitions are slightly different in meaning as illustrated by Figure 3.13. We can interpret that (a) A ∘ R seeks for output for an input A, and (b) R ∘ S is the series connection of two input–output relations R and S.

If the fuzzy set A is given in a discrete form (arrays) and fuzzy relations R and S are given in discrete expressions (i.e., fuzzy matrices), the results of composition A ∘ R and R ∘ S will be expressed by fuzzy matrices and the composition can be defined as an operation of matrices. However, the dimensions of fuzzy matrices have to be matched. For example, if the size of A is $(1 \times n)$, the dimension of the fuzzy matrix R should be $(n \times m)$ with an arbitrary integer m. The size of the resultant fuzzy matrix A ∘ R will be $(1 \times m)$. This is illustrated in the following figure.

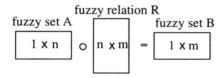

Similarly, if the size of the fuzzy matrix R is $(n \times m)$, the dimension of S should be $(m \times k)$ with an arbitrary integer k. Therefore the size of R ∘ S will be $(n \times k)$.

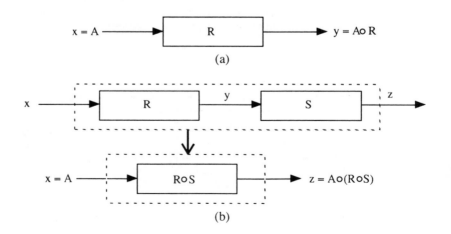

FIGURE 3.13. (a) A ∘ R and (b) R ∘ S.

The following figure represents this relation.

fuzzy relation S

fuzzy relation R ┌──────┐ fuzzy relation Ro S

┌──────┐ | | ┌──────┐
| n ✕ m | o | m ✕ k | = | n ✕ k |
└──────┘ └──────┘ └──────┘

Now I show the practical definition of the preceding two forms of composition.

Composition of fuzzy relations

> a. Let A be a fuzzy set on X, and R a fuzzy relation on X × Y. A ∘ R, the composition of A and R, is a fuzzy set on Y and its membership function is expressed as
>
> $$\mu_{A \circ R}(y) = \max_{x \in X} \left[\mu_A(x) \wedge \mu_R(x, y) \right]. \tag{3.26}$$
>
> b. Let R be a fuzzy relation on X × Y and S a fuzzy relation on Y × Z. R ∘ S, the composition of R and S, becomes a fuzzy relation on X × Z, and its membership function is given as
>
> $$\mu_{R \circ S}(x, z) = \max_{y \in Y} \left[\mu_R(x, y) \wedge \mu_S(y, z) \right]. \tag{3.27}$$

If we observe eqs. (3.26) and (3.27), we notice that both equations are organized by ∧(min) and ∨(max) operations. Therefore the preceding two composition methods are often called max-min composition. There are various other methods, for example, using multiplication instead of the min-operation, but they are beyond the scope of this book.

In usual mathematics, the definition of composition for R ⊂ X × Y and S ⊂ Y × Z is expressed such as

$$s \circ R \Leftrightarrow \{(x, y) \mid (^\exists y)(x, y) \in R \,\&\, (y, z) \in S\}.$$

However, as we can notice by comparing the preceding expression and (3. 27), in fuzzy logic we write A ∘ R and R ∘ S instead of R ∘ A and S ∘ R, by convention.

The composition by ∘ is quite similar to the multiplication of matrices. If we replace multiplication and addition with min-operation and max-operation, respectively, we obtain the composition. Let us see the following example.

Composition in comparison with matrix multiplication

> Suppose matrices R and S are as follows,
>
> $$R = \begin{bmatrix} a & b \\ c & d \end{bmatrix} \qquad S = \begin{bmatrix} e & f \\ g & h \end{bmatrix}.$$

In normal matrix multiplication RS can be calculated as

$$RS = \begin{bmatrix} a & b \\ c & d \end{bmatrix} \begin{bmatrix} e & f \\ g & h \end{bmatrix} = \begin{bmatrix} ae + bg & af + bh \\ ce + dg & cf + dh \end{bmatrix}.$$

On the other hand, the composition of fuzzy relations R ∘ S is obtained by replacing + with ∧(min) and × with ∨ so that

$$R \circ S = \begin{bmatrix} a & b \\ c & d \end{bmatrix} \circ \begin{bmatrix} e & f \\ g & h \end{bmatrix} = \begin{bmatrix} (a \wedge e) \vee (b \wedge g) & (a \wedge f) \vee (b \wedge h) \\ (c \wedge e) \vee (d \wedge g) & (c \wedge f) \vee (d \wedge h) \end{bmatrix}.$$

As we see in the preceding example, it is easy to understand the composition as a modification of matrix operations.

The properties of composition are summarized as follows.

Properties of composition

Let us consider fuzzy sets A and A′, and fuzzy relations R, R′, S, U, and T. Assume that the following conditions are satisfied.

A, A′ ⊂ X,

R, R′ ⊂ X × Y,

S, T ⊂ Y × Z,

U ⊂ Z × W.

Then the following properties are proved valid.

   i. (A ∪ A′) ∘ R = A ∘ R ∪ A′ ∘ R

  ii. (A ∩ A′) ∘ R ⊂ A ∘ R ∩ A′ ∘ R

 iii. A ∪ (R ∘ R′) = A ∘ R ∪ A ∘ R′

  iv. A ∩ (R ∘ R′) ⊂ A ∘ R ∩ A ∘ R′

   v. R ∘ S ≠ S ∘ R   (3.28)

  vi. (R ∘ S)$^{-1}$ = S^{-1} ∘ R^{-1}

 vii. R ∘ (S ∘ U) = (R ∘ S) ∘ U

viii. R ∘ (S ∩ T) = (R ∘ S) ∩ (R ∘ T)

  ix. S ⊆ T ⇒ R ∘ S ⊆ R ∘ T

EXAMPLE 3.10. COMPOSITION OF FUZZY SETS AND FUZZY RELATIONS

Suppose the universes X and Y are given as

X = {x₁, x₂, x₃}

Y = {y₁, y₂, y₃}.

If a fuzzy set A on X and a fuzzy relation R on X × Y are given such that

$$A = \begin{array}{ccc} x_1 & x_2 & x_3 \\ [0.2 & 1.0 & 0.5] \end{array}$$

$$R = \begin{array}{c} \\ x_1 \\ x_2 \\ x_3 \end{array} \begin{array}{ccc} y_1 & y_2 & y_3 \\ \begin{bmatrix} 0.8 & 0.9 & 0.1 \\ 0.6 & 1.0 & 0.5 \\ 0.2 & 0.3 & 0.9 \end{bmatrix} \end{array},$$

then composition B = A ∘ R can be calculated as

$$B = A \circ R = \begin{bmatrix} 0.2 & 1.0 & 0.5 \end{bmatrix} \circ \begin{bmatrix} 0.8 & 0.9 & 0.1 \\ 0.6 & 1.0 & 0.5 \\ 0.2 & 0.3 & 0.9 \end{bmatrix}$$

$$= [(0.2 \wedge 0.8) \vee (1.0 \wedge 0.6) \vee (0.5 \wedge 0.2),$$
$$(0.2 \wedge 0.9) \vee (1.0 \wedge 1.0) \vee (0.5 \wedge 0.3),$$
$$(0.2 \wedge 0.1) \vee (1.0 \wedge 0.5) \vee (0.5 \wedge 0.9)]$$

$$= \begin{bmatrix} 0.2 \vee 0.6 \vee 0.2 & 0.2 \vee 1.0 \vee 0.3 & 0.5 \vee 0.5 \vee 0.5 \end{bmatrix}$$

$$= \begin{array}{ccc} y_1 & y_2 & y_3 \\ [0.6 & 1.0 & 0.5]. \end{array}$$

EXAMPLE 3.11. COMPOSITION OF FUZZY RELATIONS

Let us study the problem of Example 3.2 as an example of composition of fuzzy relations.

Choose an arbitrary three cities each from New York, New Jersey, and Pennsylvania and suppose X, Y, Z are sets of cities in the respective states such as

$$X = \{x_1, x_2, x_3\}$$
$$Y = \{y_1, y_2, y_3\}$$
$$Z = \{z_1, z_2, z_3\}.$$

Let R represent a fuzzy relation of closeness between X and Y, and S a fuzzy relation of closeness of Y and Z. These fuzzy relations are given by fuzzy matrices such as

$$R = \begin{array}{c} \\ x_1 \\ x_2 \\ x_3 \end{array} \begin{array}{ccc} y_1 & y_2 & y_3 \\ \begin{bmatrix} 1 & 0.6 & 0.3 \\ 0.4 & 0.9 & 0.1 \\ 0.5 & 0.2 & 0.7 \end{bmatrix} \end{array} \qquad S = \begin{array}{c} \\ y_1 \\ y_2 \\ y_3 \end{array} \begin{array}{ccc} z_1 & z_2 & z_3 \\ \begin{bmatrix} 1 & 0.1 & 0.5 \\ 0.7 & 0.9 & 0.2 \\ 0.1 & 0.8 & 0.8 \end{bmatrix} \end{array}.$$

The composition $R \circ S$ of R and S can be calculated as

$$R \circ S = \begin{array}{c} \\ x_1 \\ x_2 \\ x_3 \end{array} \begin{array}{ccc} y_1 & y_2 & y_3 \end{array} \left[\begin{array}{ccc} 1 & 0.6 & 0.3 \\ 0.4 & 0.9 & 0.1 \\ 0.5 & 0.2 & 0.7 \end{array} \right] \qquad S = \begin{array}{c} \\ y_1 \\ y_2 \\ y_3 \end{array} \begin{array}{ccc} z_1 & z_2 & z_3 \end{array} \left[\begin{array}{ccc} 1 & 0.1 & 0.5 \\ 0.7 & 0.9 & 0.2 \\ 0.1 & 0.8 & 0.8 \end{array} \right].$$

$$= \left[\begin{array}{c} (1 \wedge 1) \vee (0.6 \wedge 0.7) \vee (0.3 \wedge 0.1) \\ (0.4 \wedge 1) \vee (0.9 \wedge 0.7) \vee (0.1 \wedge 0.1) \\ (0.5 \wedge 1) \vee (0.2 \wedge 0.7) \vee (0.7 \wedge 0.1) \end{array} \right.$$

$$\begin{array}{c} (1 \wedge 0.1) \vee (0.6 \wedge 0.9) \vee (0.3 \wedge 0.8) \\ (0.4 \wedge 0.1) \vee (0.9 \wedge 0.9) \vee (0.1 \wedge 0.8) \\ (0.5 \wedge 0.1) \vee (0.2 \wedge 0.9) \vee (0.7 \wedge 0.8) \end{array}$$

$$\left. \begin{array}{c} (1 \wedge 0.5) \vee (0.6 \wedge 0.2) \vee (0.3 \wedge 0.8) \\ (0.4 \wedge 0.5) \vee (0.9 \wedge 0.2) \vee (0.1 \wedge 0.8) \\ (0.5 \wedge 0.5) \vee (0.2 \wedge 0.2) \vee (0.7 \wedge 0.8) \end{array} \right]$$

$$= \left[\begin{array}{ccc} 1 \vee 0.6 \vee 0.1 & 0.1 \vee 0.6 \vee 0.3 & 0.5 \vee 0.2 \vee 0.3 \\ 0.4 \vee 0.7 \vee 0.1 & 0.1 \vee 0.9 \vee 0.1 & 0.4 \vee 0.2 \vee 0.1 \\ 0.5 \vee 0.2 \vee 0.1 & 0.1 \vee 0.2 \vee 0.7 & 0.5 \vee 0.2 \vee 0.7 \end{array} \right]$$

$$= \begin{array}{c} \\ x_1 \\ x_2 \\ x_3 \end{array} \begin{array}{ccc} z_1 & z_2 & z_3 \end{array} \left[\begin{array}{ccc} 1 & 0.6 & 0.5 \\ 0.7 & 0.9 & 0.4 \\ 0.5 & 0.7 & 0.7 \end{array} \right].$$

What does this $R \circ S$ mean anyway? The composition $R \circ S$ represents the closeness of X to Z, when we assume taking routes through Y. The following description is the reason for thinking in such a way.

The membership value of $R \circ S$ with respect to x_1 and z_1 is

$$\mu_{R \circ S}(x_1, z_1) = 1.$$

We can interpret this membership value as representing the closeness of x_1 and z_1. There are three routes from x_1 to z_1, by way of y_1, y_2, and y_3. This is illustrated in the following figure; the numbers on arrows show the membership values for closeness.

Closeness of each route

Route-1: $x_1 \xrightarrow{1.0} y_1 \xrightarrow{1.0} z_1$ $1.0 \wedge 1.0 = 1.0$

Route-2: $x_1 \xrightarrow{0.6} y_1 \xrightarrow{0.7} z_1$ $0.6 \wedge 0.7 = 0.6$ max $\Rightarrow 1.0$

Route-3: $x_1 \xrightarrow{0.3} y_1 \xrightarrow{0.1} z_1$ $0.3 \wedge 0.1 = 0.1$

On each route there are membership values for the closeness of X and Y and the closeness of Y and Z. We apply min-operation to obtain the total closeness. Min-operation excludes the long routes from being selected (note that the larger the value, the closer). Also, it is natural to select the shortest route of the three for "closeness." Because the shortest route has the largest membership value, we apply max-operation to select the most desirable route. Thus we get the closeness membership value of R ∘ S for x_1 and z_1 as 1.0. Applying the similar operation we obtain the fuzzy relation R ∘ S.

To program the composition on a computer, we can replace × with ∧ and + with ∨ in the multiplication of matrices.

Let us consider the composition A ∘ R of fuzzy set A and fuzzy relation R. Fuzzy set A is represented by an array of (1 × 3) elements and fuzzy relation R by a matrix of (3 × 2) elements. The resultant A ∘ R is an array of (1 × 2) elements.

fuzzy relation R

fuzzy set A

| 0.8 | 0.5 | 0.1 |

∘

1.0	0.2
0.5	0.4
0.3	0.9

fuzzy set A∘R

=

| 0.8 | 0.4 |

When we program the preceding operation, we first divide the fuzzy matrix R into two arrays R_1 and R_2.

fuzzy relation R

1.0	0.2
0.5	0.4
0.3	0.9

array R_1 array R_2

Then we calculate A ∘ R_1 and A ∘ R_2 such as

fuzzy relation R_1

fuzzy set A

| 0.8 | 0.5 | 0.1 |

A[0] A[1] A[2]

∘

R[0,0]	1.0
R[1,0]	0.5
R[2,0]	0.3

fuzzy set A∘R_1

=

| 0.8 |

Therefore

$$(0.8 \wedge 1.0) \vee (0.5 \wedge 0.5) \vee (0.1 \wedge 0.3) = 0.8 \vee 0.5 \vee 0.1 = 0.8.$$

Similarly, we obtain A ∘ R_2 = 0.4.

If we substitute those values in the array for A ∘ R, we will get

A ∘ R | 0.8 | 0.4. |

3.4 Application Examples of Fuzzy Relations

3.4.1 Guessing Game

Sally (a fictitious name) is nearsighted and colorblind. When she goes to a local grocery where fruits are placed on high shelves, she cannot see them very well. She can only recognize the size and blurred shape of the fruits. She has lived in such a world for some 20 years and now she is a housewife, and she has some knowledge about the features of the fruits. For example, tangerines are round and relatively small.

Let us represent her knowledge about fruits by a following fuzzy relation. Here we consider

fruit={tangerine, apple, pineapple, watermelon, strawberry }

shape={long, round, large }.

	tangerine	apple	pineapple	watermelon	strawberry
long	0	0	0.3	0	0.8
round	0.9	1.0	0.3	1.0	0.2
large	0.2	0.4	0.7	1.0	0.1

The preceding fuzzy relation indicates that the tangerine's likelihood of "long" is zero, "round" is 0.9, and "large" is 0.2. This represents Sally's knowledge about tangerines, that is, round and relatively small. We consider only three properties for the shape but if we increase the number, we will be more accurately representing the fuzzy relations.

Let us guess a fruit that Sally sees. If she recognizes a fruit that is "round and big" and if we can interpret this as

long   round   large
[0   0.7   1.0]

we can then guess the fruit to be the composition of fuzzy relations:

$$\begin{bmatrix} 0 & 0.7 & 1.0 \end{bmatrix} \circ \begin{bmatrix} 0 & 0 & 0.3 & 0 & 0.8 \\ 0.9 & 1.0 & 0.3 & 1.0 & 0.2 \\ 0.2 & 0.4 & 0.7 & 1.0 & 0.1 \end{bmatrix}$$

tangerine   apple   pineapple   watermelon   strawberry
= [0.7   0.7   0.7   1.0   0.2   ].

From this result, the possibility of watermelon is the highest and tangerine, apple, and pineapple come next at an equal possibility.

If Sally recognizes another fruit as "relatively long, somewhat round, and not very large," and if we can interpret her observation as

long   round   large
[0.5   0.5   0.3],

we will get the composition

$$[0.5 \quad 0.5 \quad 0.3] \circ \begin{bmatrix} 0 & 0 & 0.3 & 0 & 0.8 \\ 0.9 & 1.0 & 0.3 & 1.0 & 0.2 \\ 0.2 & 0.4 & 0.7 & 1.0 & 0.1 \end{bmatrix}$$

	tangerine	apple	pineapple	watermelon	strawberry
=	[0.5	0.5	0.3	0.5	0.5].

In this case, Sally's remark has turned out to be too ambiguous to identify the particular fruit she had in mind.

3.4.2 Matchmaking (2)

Let us view the computer-assisted matchmaking business, introduced in Section 2.5, in a different perspective.

Suppose a client P has a financial qualification for a partner such that "Even if we bought a house in Tokyo, the mortgage would be paid off within 20 years."

There are three candidates B, C, and D but the database does not show their income and we do not know what kind of house P has in mind. The only hint of being able to estimate the candidates' financial condition is through the cars they own. Their cars are priced as follows.

Name	Car's price (US$)
B	9,200
C	48,000
D	16,000

Intuition tells us P's best match is C. However, for example, let us infer who is the best match by fuzzy relations and composition.

The underlining logic in this case is

Rule 1.

IF   the car is *expensive*,

THEN   income is *high*;

Rule 2.

IF   income is *high*,

THEN   mortgage will be paid off in a *short* period.

Let us adopt the three sets involved in the reasoning:

car's price = {cheap, middle, expensive }

income = {low, average, high }

mortgage payment period = {short, average, long }.

Rule 1 represents the relation between the car's price and income and this can be expressed by the fuzzy relation

$$
R = \text{(car)}
\begin{array}{c}
\\
\text{cheap} \\
\text{middle} \\
\text{expensive}
\end{array}
\begin{array}{c}
\text{(income)} \\
\begin{array}{ccc}
\text{low} & \text{middle} & \text{high}
\end{array} \\
\begin{bmatrix}
0.6 & 0.3 & 0.3 \\
0.3 & 0.8 & 0.3 \\
0.1 & 0.3 & 0.7
\end{bmatrix}
\end{array}.
$$

The first column of the fuzzy matrix, for example, shows that low income people tend to have cheap cars, and the possibility of ownership declines as the price gets higher. The other columns are filled in with the same idea.

On the other hand, the relation between income and mortgage payment period will be given in the fuzzy relation S:

$$
S = \text{(income)}
\begin{array}{c}
\\
\text{low} \\
\text{average} \\
\text{high}
\end{array}
\begin{array}{c}
\text{(mortgage payment)} \\
\begin{array}{ccc}
\text{short} & \text{average} & \text{long}
\end{array} \\
\begin{bmatrix}
0 & 0.3 & 1.0 \\
0.2 & 0.6 & 0.5 \\
0.8 & 0.4 & 0.4
\end{bmatrix}
\end{array}.
$$

Note that the preceding fuzzy relations form such inclusion as

$R \subset$ (car's price) $\times$ (income)

$S \subset$ (income) $\times$ (mortgage payment period).

Therefore fuzzy relation $R \circ S$ obtained by the composition is a fuzzy relation on the Cartesian product of (car's price) $\times$ (mortgage payment period).

The composition $R \circ S$ will be

$$
R \circ S =
\begin{array}{c}
\\
\text{cheap} \\
\text{middle} \\
\text{expensive}
\end{array}
\begin{array}{c}
\begin{array}{ccc}
\text{low} & \text{middle} & \text{high}
\end{array} \\
\begin{bmatrix}
0.6 & 0.3 & 0.3 \\
0.3 & 0.8 & 0.3 \\
0.1 & 0.3 & 0.7
\end{bmatrix}
\end{array}
$$

$$
\circ
\begin{array}{c}
\\
\text{low} \\
\text{average} \\
\text{high}
\end{array}
\begin{array}{c}
\begin{array}{ccc}
\text{short} & \text{average} & \text{long}
\end{array} \\
\begin{bmatrix}
0 & 0.3 & 1.0 \\
0.2 & 0.6 & 0.5 \\
0.8 & 0.4 & 0.4
\end{bmatrix}
\end{array}
$$

$$
=
\begin{array}{c}
\\
\text{cheap} \\
\text{middle} \\
\text{expensive}
\end{array}
\begin{array}{c}
\begin{array}{ccc}
\text{short} & \text{average} & \text{long}
\end{array} \\
\begin{bmatrix}
0.3 & 0.3 & 0.6 \\
0.3 & 0.6 & 0.5 \\
0.7 & 0.4 & 0.4
\end{bmatrix}
\end{array}.
$$

Let us grade the three candidates' cars into cheap, middle, and high in a fuzzy matrix format such as

$$
= \begin{array}{c} \\ B \\ C \\ D \end{array} \begin{bmatrix} \overset{\text{cheap}}{0.9} & \overset{\text{middle}}{0.1} & \overset{\text{expensive}}{0} \\ 0 & 0.2 & 0.8 \\ 0.3 & 0.6 & 0.1 \end{bmatrix}.
$$

This fuzzy matrix represents the fact that B has a cheap car, D's car is more expensive, and C has the most expensive car.

The three candidates' mortgage payment periods can then be inferred by the composition as B's mortgage payment:

$$
\overset{\text{(car)}}{\begin{bmatrix} \overset{\text{cheap}}{0.9} & \overset{\text{middle}}{0.1} & \overset{\text{expensive}}{0} \end{bmatrix}} \circ \begin{bmatrix} 0.3 & 0.3 & 0.6 \\ 0.3 & 0.6 & 0.5 \\ 0.7 & 0.4 & 0.4 \end{bmatrix}
$$

(mortgage)

$$
= \begin{bmatrix} \overset{\text{short}}{0.3} & \overset{\text{average}}{0.3} & \overset{\text{long}}{0.6} \end{bmatrix}.
$$

C's mortgage payment:

$$
\overset{\text{(car)}}{\begin{bmatrix} \overset{\text{cheap}}{0} & \overset{\text{middle}}{0.2} & \overset{\text{expensive}}{0.8} \end{bmatrix}} \circ \begin{bmatrix} 0.3 & 0.3 & 0.6 \\ 0.3 & 0.6 & 0.5 \\ 0.7 & 0.4 & 0.4 \end{bmatrix}
$$

(mortgage)

$$
= \begin{bmatrix} \overset{\text{short}}{0.7} & \overset{\text{average}}{0.4} & \overset{\text{long}}{0.4} \end{bmatrix}.
$$

D's mortgage payment:

$$
\overset{\text{(car)}}{\begin{bmatrix} \overset{\text{cheap}}{0.3} & \overset{\text{middle}}{0.6} & \overset{\text{expensive}}{0.1} \end{bmatrix}} \circ \begin{bmatrix} 0.3 & 0.3 & 0.6 \\ 0.3 & 0.6 & 0.5 \\ 0.7 & 0.4 & 0.4 \end{bmatrix}
$$

(mortgage)

$$
= \begin{bmatrix} \overset{\text{short}}{0.3} & \overset{\text{average}}{0.6} & \overset{\text{long}}{0.5} \end{bmatrix}.
$$

If we compare the results of composition, we notice that B needs a long period of mortgage payments for a house, and that D also needs a somewhat longer time than average, whereas C can pay off the mortgage in a short period of time. Thus it is obvious that C is the closest to qualify as P's candidate for marriage.

References

[1] Zadeh, L. A. 1973. Outline of a new approach to the analysis of complex systems and decision process. *IEEE Transactions on Systems, Man, and Cybernetics*, 3, 1; 28–44.
[2] Zimmermann, H. J. 1991. *Fuzzy Set Theory and Its Applications*, 2nd ed., Norwell, MA: Kluwer Academic.

4

Fuzzy Reasoning

In this chapter, fuzzy reasoning is described. First, fuzzy reasoning is introduced, and the reasoning mechanism is described in detail. Then various forms of fuzzy reasoning are given.

4.1 Classification of Fuzzy Reasoning

We need inference rules to perform fuzzy reasoning. Inference rules for fuzzy reasoning are expressed in IF-THEN format. IF-THEN rules used in fuzzy reasoning are called "fuzzy IF-THEN rules."

Fuzzy reasoning methods are roughly classified in Figure 4.1.

We can classify fuzzy reasoning methods into direct methods and indirect methods. Most popular reasoning methods are direct methods. Indirect methods conduct reasoning by truth-value space. Although indirect methods are technically interesting, they have a relatively complex reasoning mechanism and are beyond the scope of this book.

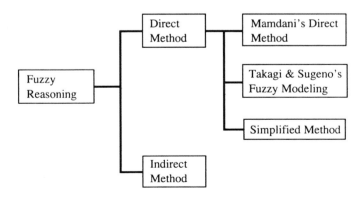

FIGURE 4.1. Classification of fuzzy reasoning.

The most popular of the direct methods was first proposed by Mamdani [1;5]. Mamdani's direct method has a simple structure of min- and max-operations and is, therefore, very popular in applications.

At the time of this writing, there are many other reasoning methods that improve upon Mamdani's direct method. In this book we look at two representing methods in addition to Mamdani's method: using linear functions in the consequence part, and simplifying the consequence part into constants altogether.

Let us first look at Mamdani's direct method. Direct methods use an inference rule such as:

IF x is A and y is B THEN z is C

where A, B, and C are fuzzy sets.

In the IF-THEN rule the term following the IF statement is called the premise, and the term following THEN is called the consequence. Variables x and y, used in the premise part, are called premise variables and the variable z, found in the consequence part, is called a consequence variable.

Let us apply the preceding format to a practical rule. For example,

IF   room temperature is "a little high"

AND   humidity is "quite high,"

THEN   increase the air conditioner setting to "High."

When we compare this rule with the preceding form, we find the correspondence:

x: room temperature

y: humidity

z: air conditioner setting

A: a little high

B: quite high

C: high.

Here A, B, and C are fuzzy sets. Room temperature is measured in Celsius, humidity in percent, and we assume the air conditioner's temperature setting is in 10 different levels from 0 to 10 with a higher number corresponding to greater effect.

If we replace the fuzzy sets "a little high," "quite high," and "high" with more explicit fuzzy numbers such as "about 20 degrees," "about 80%," and "about 8," respectively, we can rewrite the preceding rule as

IF   x is "about 20 degrees"

AND   y is "about 80%,"

THEN   z is "about 8."

Next, I describe another fuzzy reasoning method that uses linear functions in the consequence part. This method uses linear functions, which represent input-output relations, instead of fuzzy sets for the consequence part of the fuzzy rule such as:

IF x is A and y is B THEN $z = ax + by + c$.

Here, a, b, and c are the parameters of the linear function in the consequence part, and they are called the consequence part parameters. The linear equation in the consequence part is called the consequence part linear equation.

The preceding air conditioner rule can be written in this form such as

IF   room temperature is "a little high"

AND   humidity is "quite high,"

THEN   air conditioner setting

= room temperature × 0.2 + humidity × 0.05.

We can interpret the consequence part linear equation in the preceding rule as follows.

First, we rewrite this equation as

air conditioner setting = 0.05 × (room temperature × 4.0 + humidity).

This equation shows that the room temperature has four times more weight than humidity. 0.05 is multiplied to scale the value to the level of the air conditioner setting (0–10).

Therefore we can further rewrite the rule in a more practical form such as

IF   x is "about 20 degrees"

AND   y is "about 80%,"

THEN   z = 0.2x + 0.05y.

In general, it is difficult to determine the linear equations for the consequence part empirically. In this type of reasoning method, we are assumed to apply modeling techniques using input-output data to obtain rules. Therefore this reasoning method is sometimes referred to as fuzzy modeling.

Another popular approach for fuzzy reasoning uses a simplified consequence part. This is a special case of fuzzy reasoning of the two methods previously mentioned. In this method the rule will be written as follows:

IF x is A and y is B THEN $z = c$.

Here c is a real value. This real value can be considered as a special fuzzy set without vagueness, and sometimes it is called "a fuzzy singleton." In a different point of view, only the constant term exists in the linear equation for the simplified method.

In the simplified method, the afore-mentioned air conditioner example may be written as

IF   room temperature is "a little high"

AND   humidity is "quite high,"

THEN   air conditioner setting $= 8$.

Note that in the first method, the consequence part uses a fuzzy set "about 8."
We can further rewrite the rule in a more practical form such as

IF   x is "about 20 degrees"

AND   y is "about 80%,"

THEN $z = 8$.

The details of Mamdani's direct method, the method that uses linear functions for the consequence part, and the simplified method are given in Sections 4.3, 4.4, and 4.5 respectively.

4.2 Mechanism of Fuzzy Reasoning

I have introduced the three types of fuzzy reasoning methods in the previous section. We can discuss their mechanisms in the same framework. In this section, I show the unified view of fuzzy reasoning methods integrating those three methods. Individual methods are discussed in Section 4.3.

In conventional (binary) logic, reasoning is based on "modus ponens" (deduction) and "modus tollens" (induction). These two are complementary. In modus ponens, when the statement "If A, then B" is true, we infer "If A is true, then B is true." We write this reasoning as

premise 1: $A \rightarrow B$

premise 2: A

_____

consequence: B

where operation $\rightarrow$ means implication.
We can rewrite this condition in an IF-THEN form such as

premise 1:   IF x is A   THEN y is B

premise 2:   x is A

_____

consequence: y is B.

In binary logic A and B are crisp sets.
On the other hand, in modus tollens, when the statement "If A, then B" is true, we infer "If A is not true, then B is not true." The reasoning process is written as

premise 1: $A \rightarrow B$

premise 2:   not A

_____

consequence: not B.

Let us see a practical example of modus ponens in a rule form.

premise 1:   IF temperature is less than 10°C THEN turn up heater.
premise 2:   Temperature is 5°C (temperature is less than 10°C).

---

consequence: Turn up heater.

Premise 2, "temperature is 5°C," completely satisfies the condition of premise 1 "temperature is less than 10°C," and thus we conclude "turn up heater." This conclusion is derived by conventional binary logic.

Fuzzy reasoning is based on the generalized modus ponens (GMP). The generalized modus ponens may be also called "fuzzy modus ponens." If we write a generalized modus ponens in IF-THEN form, we get

premise 1:   IF x is A   THEN y is B
premise 2:   x is A'

---

consequence: y is B'

where A, A', B, and B' are fuzzy sets.

A major difference from the modus ponens based on binary logic is that in the generalized modus ponens, we can use a different fuzzy set for A in premise 1 and A' in premise 2. In binary logic, crisp set A in premise 1 and premise 2 must be completely identical.

On the other hand, in the generalized modus ponens based on fuzzy logic, fuzzy sets A and A' in premise 1 and premise 2 do not have to be precisely the same. We can still infer the conclusion "y is B'" from the premise "y is B" depending on their similarity. This is why fuzzy reasoning is sometimes called "approximate reasoning."

Human reasoning is closer to fuzzy reasoning. For example, if we apply fuzzy reasoning to the preceding example of temperature and heater, we get

premise 1:   IF   room temperature is low   THEN turn up heater.
premise 2:   Temperature is rather low.

---

consequence: Turn up heater considerably.

In the generalized modus ponens, we can conclude to "turn up heater considerably" from the rule of premise 1 "IF room temperature is low THEN turn up heater" and the condition "temperature is rather low." To be more exact, if we have only one rule in premise 1, such flexible reasoning is impossible. In ordinary fuzzy reasoning, we need multiple rules in premise 1 to perform flexible reasoning. The details are described in Section 4.3 and later.

Practical fuzzy reasoning is composed of the following steps.

Step 1.
Measure the adaptability of the premise of rules for a given input.

Step 2.
From the adaptability obtained in the preceding, infer the conclusion of each rule.

Step 3.
Aggregate the individual conclusions to obtain the overall conclusion.

4.3 Method 1: Mamdani's Direct Method

Section 4.3.1 describes the mechanism of Mamdani's direct method and Section 4.3.2 shows how to materialize fuzzy reasoning by fuzzy relations. Section 4.3.3 shows some ways to compose fuzzy relations based on various implications.

4.3.1 Mechanism of Reasoning

First we look at the mechanism of the reasoning method by using a simple example with two rules given by (4.1). (4.1) has two variables in the premise part and one variable in the consequence part, and we can call it a two-input one-output IF-THEN rule.

$$
\begin{array}{llllllll}
\text{Rule 1:} & \text{IF} & x \text{ is } A_1 & \text{and} & y \text{ is } B_1 & \text{THEN} & z \text{ is } C_1 \\
\text{Rule 2:} & \text{IF} & x \text{ is } A_2 & \text{and} & y \text{ is } B_2 & \text{THEN} & z \text{ is } C_2
\end{array}
\tag{4.1}
$$

where A_1, A_2, B_1, B_2, C_1, and C_2 are fuzzy sets. Figure 4.2 shows the reasoning process.

Now let us suppose x_0 and y_0 to be the input for the premise part variables x and y, respectively. Let us denote this input as (x_0, y_0). Reasoning process for the input (x_0, y_0) will be as follows.

Step 1.
Measure the adaptability of each rule for the input (x_0, y_0) such that:

$$
\begin{array}{ll}
\text{Adaptability of Rule 1:} & W_1 = \mu_{A_1}(x_0) \wedge \mu_{B_1}(y_0) \\
\text{Adaptability of Rule 2:} & W_2 = \mu_{A_2}(x_0) \wedge \mu_{B_2}(y_0).
\end{array}
\tag{4.2}
$$

In the rules of (4.1), there are two variables x and y, in the premise part. Accordingly, we can obtain two membership values for the two-input x_0, y_0. If we apply min-operation, represented by $\wedge$, to the preceding membership values, we will get the adaptability of each rule.

Let us extend this procedure to the general case. If there is m input, the IF-THEN rule includes the premise such as

$$x_1 \text{ is } A_1 \quad \text{and} \ldots \text{ and } \quad x_m \text{ is } A_m.$$

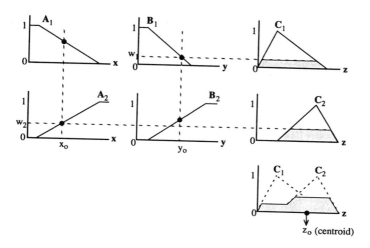

FIGURE 4.2. Reasoning process of Mamdani's direct method.

The adaptability of the premise part will then be given by

$$\mu_{A_1}(x_1) \wedge \cdots \wedge \mu_{A_m}(y_m).$$

Step 2.

Apply the adaptability obtained in Step 1 to the fuzzy sets in the consequence part and obtain the conclusion of each rule.

Conclusion of Rule 1: $\mu_{C'_1}(x_0) = W_1 \wedge \mu_{C_1}(z) \quad \forall z \in Z$
Conclusion of Rule 2: $\mu_{C'_2}(x_0) = W_2 \wedge \mu_{C_2}(z) \quad \forall z \in Z.$ (4.3)

(4.3) uses $\wedge$(min) operation but this may be different due to different implication. The calculation of (4.3) corresponds with cutting the fuzzy sets in the consequence part by the height of the adaptability of the premise in Figure 4.2 (the result is the shaded area).

Step 3.

Aggregate the conclusion of each rule obtained in Step 2 and make the final conclusion as follows.

Final conclusion $\mu_C(z) = \mu_{C'_1}(z) \vee \mu_{C'_2}(z).$ (4.4)

(4.4) is an example of two rules. In general. with n rules, (4.4) can be written such as

$$\mu_C(z) = \mu_{C'_1}(z) \vee \mu_{C'_2}(z) \vee \cdots \vee \mu_{C'_n}(z).$$

This completes the reasoning process. Multiplication can be alternatively used for the preceding $\wedge$(min) operation.

Note that the final conclusion is given by a fuzzy set in Step 3. This is not practical when we need a definite value as an output of reasoning such as in process control.

Therefore we have to convert the fuzzy set to a definite value. The operation to convert a fuzzy set into a definite value is called "defuzzification." In Figure 4.2 I assigned z_0 for the definite value obtained by defuzzification.

Commonly used methods for defuzzification are as follows.

  i. Take the center of gravity of the fuzzy set for conclusion

$$z_0 = \frac{\int \mu_C(z)z\,dz}{\int \mu_C(z)\,dz} \tag{4.5}$$

where $\int$ means ordinary integral.

 ii. Take the maximum value of membership in the fuzzy set for conclusion

$$z_0 = \left(\max_z \mu_C(z) \right).$$

There is a variety of defuzzification methods proposed but they produce little difference in practice, so they are not mentioned here.

The preceding reasoning process assumed definite input x_0, y_0. There may be cases when the input is given by fuzzy sets A', B'. In such cases, the calculation of adaptability in Step 1 may be replaced with the following Step $1'$.

Adaptability of Rule 1:

$$W_1 = \left(\max_x \left(\mu_{A_1}(x) \wedge \mu_{A'}(x) \right) \right) \wedge \left(\max_y \left(\mu_{B_1}(y) \wedge \mu_{B'}(y) \right) \right).$$

Adaptability of Rule 2:

$$W_2 = \left(\max_x \left(\mu_{A_2}(x) \wedge \mu_{A'}(x) \right) \right) \wedge \left(\max_y \left(\mu_{B_2}(y) \wedge \mu_{B'}(y) \right) \right).$$

Figure 4.3 shows an example of such a calculation.

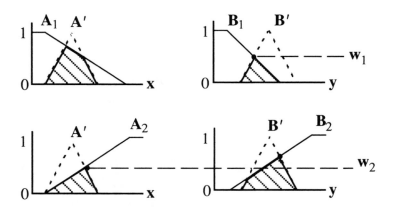

FIGURE 4.3. Calculation of adaptability when input is fuzzy set.

EXAMPLE 4.1. AUTOMOTIVE DRIVING LOGIC CONSIDERING SPEED AND DISTANCE BETWEEN CARS

Let us apply fuzzy logic to an automotive driving situation considering speed and distance between cars. Assume the following rules for this logic.

Rule 1:   IF   distance between cars is short

AND   speed is slow,

THEN   hold the gas pedal steady (maintain the speed).

Rule 2:   IF   distance between cars is short

AND   speed is fast,

THEN   step on the brake (reduce the speed).

Rule 3:   IF   distance between cars is long

AND   speed is slow,

THEN   step on the gas pedal (increase the speed).

Rule 4:   IF   distance between cars is long

AND   speed is fast,

THEN   hold the gas pedal steady (maintain the speed).

The preceding rules are written in ordinary words, and we cannot directly apply fuzzy logic. We first have to express the necessary information such as "short," "long," "slow," and "step on brake" by fuzzy sets. In this example, these fuzzy sets can be represented by the membership functions shown in Figure 4.4. For the adjustment of speed, we use the increment of speed (acceleration) as a variable.

These membership functions need to be defined appropriately for the situations under consideration. For example, the speed of 70 km/h would be "fast" on an urban street but it would be "slow" on a highway.

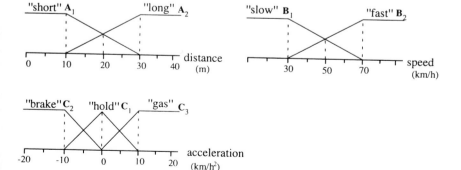

FIGURE 4.4. Membership functions for driving.

Let us put

x: distance between cars

y: speed

z: speed adjustment (gas pedal or brake operation).

The respective total sets can be defined as

$X = \{x \mid 0 \le x \le 40\}$ [m]
$Y = \{y \mid 0 \le y \le 100\}$ [km/h]
$Z = \{z \mid -20 \le z \le 20\}$ [km/h^2].

The preceding regions can be determined by common sense. For example, the distance between cars and the speed cannot take negative values. There are certain upper bounds on the distance between cars and there is a speed limit on a road.

Now let us label each fuzzy set.

A_1:   "short" (distance between cars)

A_2:   "long" (distance between cars)

B_1:   "slow" (speed)

B_2:   "fast" (speed)

C_1:   "maintain" (speed)

C_2:   "reduce" (speed)

C_3:   "increase" (speed)

Then the preceding rules written in ordinary words can be rewritten in the IF-THEN form such as

Rule 1   IF   x is A_1 and   y is B_1 THEN   z is C_1;
Rule 2   IF   x is A_1 and   y is B_2 THEN   z is C_2;
Rule 3   IF   x is A_2 and   y is B_1 THEN   z is C_3;
Rule 4   IF   x is A_2 and   y is B_2 THEN   z is C_1.

We can also express these rules as the rule table shown in Figure 4.5.

For example, the shaded portion of the table represents a rule

IF   x is A_1 and y is B_1 THEN   z is C_1

y \ x	B_1	B_2
A_1	C_1	C_2
A_2	C_3	C_1

FIGURE 4.5. Rule table for driving.

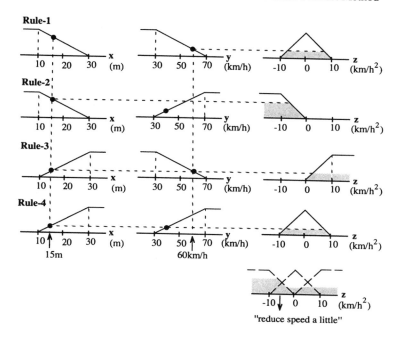

FIGURE 4.6. Reasoning process.

and corresponds with Rule 1. As the number of rules increases, it can become more and more difficult to see individual rules in a sequential order. In such a case, it is better to summarize the rules into a rule table.

Figure 4.6 shows the reasoning process. This figure shows the reasoning process for the distance between cars as 15 m and the speed of 60 km/h as input. The conclusions will lie somewhere between "keep speed" and "reduce speed" and this can be expressed linguistically as "reduce speed somewhat."

The comparison of membership functions in Figure 4.4 and the actual input will give us the validity of the reasoning. First, let us consider the distance between cars. The input of 15 m for the distance between the cars gives the membership values of 0.75 and 0.25 for the fuzzy sets "short" and "long," respectively. If we use linguistic expression, 15 m for the distance between the cars will be "somewhat short." The speed input of 60 km/h will be "somewhat fast." Summarizing these two we get the expression "the distance between the cars is somewhat short and the speed is somewhat fast." By comparing the linguistic input and the linguistic rules, we can judge that the conclusion "reduce speed somewhat" should be valid. In such ways, comparing the given rules and given input, fuzzy reasoning can infer a conclusion by interpolation as is done ordinarily.

4.3.2 Fuzzy Relations and Compositional Rule of Inference

In Section 4.3.1 we looked into the mechanism of Mamdani's direct method. If we program this mechanism, we can materialize the fuzzy reasoning on a computer. In Section 4.3.2 I show that we can also apply fuzzy relations to realize the direct method of fuzzy reasoning.

Because neither approach is perfect, we should adopt a method that better suits the objective. If the number of rules is large, it is better to apply a fuzzy relations approach for computer programs. Whatever the number of rules, IF-THEN rules would fit into the compact fuzzy relation form. Such fit-in operation is done offline, and once we obtain the compact form, the speed of reasoning can be higher than the approach of 4.3.1. However, it takes time to fit the IF-THEN rules into a compact form. If the number of rules is small, it is simpler to program the approach of 4.3.1 directly.

The fuzzy relations approach for the direct method of fuzzy reasoning involves the following steps.

Step 1.
Convert IF-THEN rules into fuzzy relations.

Step 2.
Obtain conclusion using the preceding fuzzy relations and the compositional rule of inference.

Let us review the generalized modus ponens described in Section 4.2. The form was:

premise 1:	IF x is A	THEN y is B
premise 2:	x is A$'$	(4.6)

-----

consequence:	y is B$'$

where A, A$'$, B, and B$'$ are fuzzy sets. (4.6) shows how to infer "y is B$'$" when the condition "x is A$'$" is given for the rule "IF x is A THEN y is B."

In the fuzzy relations approach, we first convert the IF-THEN rule in premise 1 into the fuzzy relation $R_{A \to B}$. Then the conclusion B$'$ will be inferred from the fuzzy relations $R_{A \to B}$ and A$'$ of premise 2, applying the compositional operation such as

$$B' = A' \circ R_{A \to B}. \qquad (4.7)$$

The reasoning process based on (4.7) is called the compositional rule of inference. The compositional operation ∘ was introduced in Section 3.3. Figure 4.7 shows the reasoning mechanism using fuzzy relations and the compositional rule of inference.

In the following text, we first look into the method to convert IF-THEN rules to fuzzy relations and then how to obtain a conclusion using fuzzy relations and the compositional rule of inference.

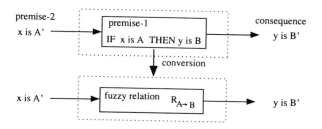

FIGURE 4.7. Fuzzy reasoning by fuzzy relations and the compositional rule of inference.

4.3.2.a Conversion of IF-THEN Rules to Fuzzy Relations

In this section the premise "IF x is A THEN y is B" is simply written as A → B. A → B shows the relation between A and B, and it can be converted to a fuzzy relation. The conversion methods depend on how the implication A → B is to be interpreted. The details of implications are given in Section 4.3.3. In this section I introduce the conversion methods proposed by Zadeh and Mamdani. In the following context × operation means the Cartesian product.

Conversion to fuzzy relations

- Zadeh's method: Zadeh proposed the following method to compose fuzzy relations R:

$$R = A \rightarrow B = (X \times B) \oplus (\overline{A} \times Y)$$
$$= \int_{X \times Y} 1 \wedge \left(1 - \mu_A(x) + \mu_B(y)\right) / (x, y). \qquad (4.8)$$

Here ⊕ means the bounded sum. The bounded sum is defined as

$$\mu_{A \oplus B}(x) = 1 \wedge (\mu_A(x) + \mu_B(x)).$$

This conversion method is based on Lukasiewicz's implication defined by

$$a \rightarrow b = (1 - a + b) \wedge 1. \qquad (4.9)$$

- Mamdani's method: Mamdani proposed the following method to compose fuzzy relations R.

$$R = A \rightarrow B = A \times B$$
$$= \int_{X \times Y} \left(\mu_A(x) \wedge \mu_B(y)\right) / (x, y). \qquad (4.10)$$

This conversion is based on the definition of Cartesian product such as

$$a \rightarrow b = a \wedge b. \qquad (4.11)$$

It is more common to use Mamdani's conversion method for fuzzy relations because it is easier to calculate (4.10) than (4.8) and the method better matches intuition.

We can rewrite the preceding conversion method by membership value form such as

---

Zadeh's method:

$$\mu_R(x, y) = 1 \wedge \left(1 - \mu_A(x) + \mu_B(y)\right).$$

Mamdani's method:

$$\mu_R(x, y) = \mu_A(x) \wedge \mu_B(y).$$

Next, let us consider a fuzzy reasoning with two propositions such as (4.12).

$$\text{IF} \quad x \text{ is } A \quad \text{and } y \text{ is } B \quad \text{THEN } z \text{ is } C \tag{4.12}$$

where A, B, and C are the fuzzy subsets of X, Y, and Z, respectively.
Let (4.12) be simplified as

$A \text{ and } B \rightarrow C.$

However, it is not exact to express the preceding relation as

$A \cap B \rightarrow C$

because A and B are subsets of different sets X and Y, respectively. If the $\cap$ operation is indispensable we should apply the cylindrical extension shown in Example 3.5 of Section 3.1.2 such as

$$\text{"x is A and y is B"} \Leftrightarrow (x, y) \text{ is } (A \times Y) \cap (X \times B)$$

$$(x, y) \text{ is } A \times B. \tag{4.13}$$

If we apply (4.13), the fuzzy relation "A and B" can be expressed as

$A \text{ and } B = A \times B$

$$= \int_{X \times Y} \left(\mu_A(x) \wedge \mu_B(y)\right) / (x, y). \tag{4.14}$$

Hence the rule "$A \text{ and } B \rightarrow C$" can be translated as follows.

Composition of complex fuzzy relations

- Zadeh's method:

$$R = A \text{ and } B \rightarrow C$$

$$= (X \times Y \times C) \oplus \overline{(A \times B \times Z)}$$

$$= \int_{X \times Y \times Z} 1 \wedge \left(1 - (\mu_A(x) \wedge \mu_B(y)) + \mu_C(z)\right) / (x, y, z) \tag{4.15}$$

- Mamdani's method:

$$R = A \ and \ B \to C$$

$$= A \times B \times C$$

$$= \int_{X \times Y \times Z} \left(\mu_A(x) \wedge \mu_B(y) \wedge \mu_C(z) \right) \big/ (x, y, z). \qquad (4.16)$$

If we express the preceding methods of conversion by membership values, we get:

Zadeh's method:

$$\mu_R(x, y, z) = 1 \wedge \left(1 - \left(\mu_A(x) \wedge \mu_B(y) \right) + \mu_C(z) \right).$$

Mamdani's method:

$$\mu_R(x, y, z) = \mu_A(x) \wedge \mu_B(y) \wedge \mu_C(z).$$

Let us extend the preceding discussion to the general case. When the IF-THEN rule is written such as

$$x \ is \ A_1 \quad and \dots \quad and \ x_m \ is \ A_m \to C,$$

Zadeh's conversion formula gives

$$= \int_{X_1 \times \dots \times X_M \times Z} 1 \wedge \frac{\left\{ 1 - \left(\mu_{A_1}(x_1) \wedge \dots \wedge \mu_{A_m}(x_m) \right) + \mu_C(z) \right\}}{(x_1, \dots, x_m, z)}.$$

Here, A_1, A_m, and C are fuzzy sets on X_1, X_m, and Z, respectively.

On the other hand, Mamdani's formula gives

$$\int_{X_1 \times \dots \times X_m \times Z} \left(\mu_{A_1}(x_1) \wedge \dots \wedge \mu_{A_m}(x_m) \wedge \mu_C(z) \right) / (x_1, \dots, x_m, z).$$

The preceding discussions are concerned with the method of converting one rule into one fuzzy relation. However, it is customary to process fuzzy reasoning with multiple rules, so following is a description of the method of composition of fuzzy relations for multiple rules.

Let us suppose there are n IF-THEN rules such as

Rule 1:   IF   x is A_1 THEN   y is B_1

Rule 2:   IF   x is A_2 THEN   y is B_2

. . .

Rule $(n-1)$:   IF   x is A_{n-1} THEN   y is B_{n-1}

Rule n: IF   x is A_n THEN   y is B_n

We can rewrite the preceding rules as follows.

$A_1 \rightarrow B_1$ else

$A_2 \rightarrow B_2$ else

$\cdots$

$A_{n-1} \rightarrow B_{n-1}$ else

$A_n \rightarrow B_n$

Here, we assume that the rules are connected by "else."

Then we convert the preceding n rules into n fuzzy relations separately such as

Rule		Fuzzy relations
$A_1 \rightarrow B_1$	else	$\Rightarrow R_1$
$A_2 \rightarrow B_2$	else	$\Rightarrow R_2$
$\cdots$		
$A_{n-1} \rightarrow B_{n-1}$	else	$\Rightarrow R_{n-1}$
$A_n \rightarrow B_n$		$\Rightarrow R_n$

Now let us compile the individual fuzzy relations into one. A problem is how to interpret the connective "else." We must take care because the interpretation depends on the method used in composing fuzzy relations. For example, in Mamdani's method, "else" is interpreted as an OR operation, whereas in Zadeh's method it is taken as an AND operation.

Compilation of fuzzy relations

With n number of rules, the fuzzy relation R_i is made from the implication $A_i \rightarrow B_i$ $(i = 1, \ldots, n)$. The compiled fuzzy relation R is given as

Mamdani's method:

$$R = R_1 \cup R_2 \cup \cdots \cup R_n = \bigcup_{i=1}^{n} R_i. \tag{4.17a}$$

Zadeh's method:

$$R = R_1 \cap R_2 \cap \cdots \cap R_n = \bigcap_{i=1}^{n} R_i. \tag{4.17b}$$

The difference in interpretation results from the difference in the method of converting rules to fuzzy relations. Let us compare Zadeh's method and Mamdani's method.

In Mamdani's method, the fuzzy relation $R = A \rightarrow B$ is given by

$$\mu_R(x, y) = \mu_A(x) \wedge \mu_B(y).$$

Substituting $\mu_A(x) = 0$, we get $\mu_R(x, y) = 0$ independently of the value of $\mu_B(y)$. Then we interpret the connective "else" as OR.

$\mu_A(x) = 0$ means the premise of the rule $A \to B$ is zero.

On the other hand, in Zadeh's method, the fuzzy relation $R = A \to B$ is given by

$$\mu_R(x, y) = 1 \wedge \left(1 - \mu_A(x) + \mu_B(y)\right).$$

Substituting $\mu_A(x) = 0$, we get $\mu_R(x, y) = 1$ independently of the value of $\mu_B(y)$. Therefore we interpret the connective "else" as AND.

Other methods of conversion fall into the category of either Zadeh's or Mamdani's. We have to select an adequate compilation method for each particular method.

EXAMPLE 4.2. COMPOSITION OF FUZZY RELATIONS

In this example, I show how to convert fuzzy IF-THEN rules into fuzzy relations, based on Zadeh's and Mamdani's method, in the following cases.

Case 1   Premises with one input variable;

Case 2   Premises with two different variables.

Case 1. Premises with one input variable.
   Consider the following rules:

Rule 1:   IF   x is A_1 THEN   y is B_1

Rule 2:   IF   x is A_2 THEN   y is B_2

where

$X = \{x_1, x_2, x_3\}$ and $A_1, A_2 \subset X$
$Y = \{y_1, y_2, y_3\}$ and $B_1, B_2 \subset Y$.

Fuzzy sets A_1, A_2, B_1, and B_2 are given as follows:

$A_1 = 1.0/x_1 + 0.6/x_2$
$A_2 = 0.8/x_2 + 1.0/X_3$
$B_1 = 1.0/y_1 + 0.6/y_2 + 0.1/y_3$
$B_2 = 0.2/y_1 + 0.8/y_2 + 0.9/y_3$

Figure 4.8 shows the preceding fuzzy sets.

• Mamdani's method
   First, let us introduce fuzzy relations using Mamdani's method. Using (4.10) we convert the rule

Rule 1 $A_1 \to B_1$

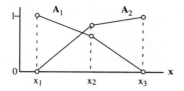 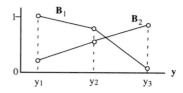

FIGURE 4.8. Fuzzy sets for Example 4.2.

into fuzzy relation R_1

$$
R_1 = \begin{array}{cc}
 & \begin{array}{ccc} \mu_{B_1}(y_1) & \mu_{B_1}(y_2) & \mu_{B_1}(y_3) \\ 1.0 & 0.6 & 0.1 \end{array} \\
\begin{array}{cc} \mu_{A_1}(x_1) & 1.0 \\ \mu_{A_1}(x_2) & 0.6 \\ \mu_{A_1}(x_3) & 0 \end{array} & \left[\begin{array}{ccc} 1.0 & 0.6 & 0.1 \\ 0.6 & 0.6 & 0.1 \\ 0 & 0 & 0 \end{array}\right]
\end{array}.
$$

In the preceding expression of R_1, membership values are added on the top and left of the fuzzy matrix for the reader's comprehension. Each element of the fuzzy matrix R_1 is calculated by Mamdani's implication. For example, the element $R_1(1, 1) = 1.0$ is given as

$$\mu_{A_1}(x_1) \wedge \mu_{B_1}(y_1) = 1.0 \wedge 1.0 = 1.0.$$

Applying the same calculation for all the combinations of x_1–x_3 and y_1–y_3, we get the preceding fuzzy relation matrix R_1. R_2, corresponding with Rule 2, can be obtained in the same way as

$$
R_2 = \begin{array}{cc}
 & \begin{array}{ccc} \mu_{B_2}(y_1) & \mu_{B_2}(y_2) & \mu_{B_2}(y_3) \\ 0.2 & 0.8 & 0.9 \end{array} \\
\begin{array}{cc} \mu_{A_2}(x_1) & 0 \\ \mu_{A_2}(x_2) & 0.8 \\ \mu_{A_2}(x_3) & 1.0 \end{array} & \left[\begin{array}{ccc} 0 & 0 & 0 \\ 0.2 & 0.8 & 0.8 \\ 0.2 & 0.8 & 0.9 \end{array}\right]
\end{array}.
$$

Compiling R_2 and R_2 by (4.17a) we get

$$R = R_1 \cup R_2 = \begin{bmatrix} 1.0 & 0.6 & 0.1 \\ 0.6 & 0.8 & 0.8 \\ 0.2 & 0.8 & 0.9 \end{bmatrix}.$$

• Zadeh's method

We can convert Rule 1 by (4.8) into the fuzzy relation R_1 such as

$$
R_1 = \begin{array}{cc}
 & \begin{array}{ccc} \mu_{B_1}(y_1) & \mu_{B_1}(y_2) & \mu_{B_1}(y_3) \\ 1.0 & 0.6 & 0.1 \end{array} \\
\begin{array}{cc} \mu_{A_1}(x_1) & 1.0 \\ \mu_{A_1}(x_2) & 0.6 \\ \mu_{A_1}(x_3) & 0 \end{array} & \left[\begin{array}{ccc} 1.0 & 0.6 & 0.1 \\ 0.6 & 1.0 & 0.5 \\ 1.0 & 1.0 & 1.0 \end{array}\right]
\end{array}
$$

where the first element is, for example, calculated by Zadeh's implication such as

$$\mu_{R_{11}} = 1 \wedge \left(1 - \mu_{A_1}(x) + \mu_{B_1}(y)\right) = 1 \wedge (1 - 1.0 + 1.0) = 1.0.$$

Applying the same calculation for all the combination of x_1-x_3 and y_1-y_3, we get the preceding fuzzy relation matrix R_1. R_2 can be obtained in the same way as

$$R_2 = \begin{matrix} & & \mu_{B_2}(y_1) & \mu_{B_2}(y_2) & \mu_{B_2}(y_3) \\ & & 0.2 & 0.8 & 0.9 \\ \mu_{A_2}(x_1) & 0 \\ \mu_{A_2}(x_2) & 0.8 \\ \mu_{A_2}(x_3) & 1.0 \end{matrix} \begin{bmatrix} 1.0 & 1.0 & 1.0 \\ 0.4 & 1.0 & 1.0 \\ 0.2 & 0.8 & 0.9 \end{bmatrix}.$$

Compiling R_1 and R_2 by (4.17b) we get

$$R = R_1 \cap R_2 = \begin{bmatrix} 1.0 & 0.6 & 0.1 \\ 0.4 & 1.0 & 0.5 \\ 0.2 & 0.8 & 0.9 \end{bmatrix}.$$

Case 2. Premises with two different variables.
Let us consider the following rules with two variables in the premise part.

Rule 1   IF   x is A_1 and   y is B_1 THEN   z is C_1

Rule 2   IF   x is A_1 and   y is B_2 THEN   z is C_2

where

$X = \{x_1, x_2, x_3\}$ and $A_1, A_2 \subset X$

$Y = \{y_1, y_2, y_3\}$ and $B_1, B_2 \subset Y$

$Z = \{z_1, z_2, z_3\}$ and $C_1, C_2 \subset Y$.

Fuzzy sets A_1, A_2, B_1, B_2, C_1, and C_2 are given as follows.

$A_1 = 1.0/x_1 + 0.6/x_2$

$A_2 = 0.8/x_2 + 1.0/x_3$

$B_1 = 1.0/y_1 + 0.5/y_2$

$B_2 = 0.2/y_2 + 0.9/y_3$

$C_1 = 1.0/z_1 + 0.6/z_2 + 0.1/z_3$

$C_2 = 0.2/z_1 + 0.8/z_2 + 0.9/z_3$

Let us convert the preceding rules into fuzzy relations using Mamdani's method. Rule 1 is written as

A_1 and $B_1 \rightarrow C_1$.

This can be converted into a fuzzy relation using Mamdani's method as follows.

Rule 1 — $\mu_{C_1}(z_1) = 1.0$:

	$\mu_{B_1}(y_1)$	$\mu_{B_1}(y_2)$	$\mu_{B_1}(y_3)$
	1.0	0.5	0
$\mu_{A_1}(x_1)$ 1.0	1.0	0.5	0
$\mu_{A_1}(x_2)$ 0.6	0.6	0.5	0
$\mu_{A_1}(x_3)$ 0	0	0	0

$\mu_{C_1}(z_2) = 0.6$:

	$\mu_{B_1}(y_1)$	$\mu_{B_1}(y_2)$	$\mu_{B_1}(y_3)$
	1.0	0.5	0
	0.6	0.5	0
	0.6	0.5	0
	0	0	0

$\mu_{C_1}(z_3) = 0.1$:

	$\mu_{B_1}(y_1)$	$\mu_{B_1}(y_2)$	$\mu_{B_1}(y_3)$
	1.0	0.5	0
	0.1	0.1	0
	0.1	0.1	0
	0	0	0

Note that the fuzzy relation is three-dimensional if the rules contain two propositions in the premises. The first element of the fuzzy matrix is calculated by Mamdani's implication such that

$$\mu_{A_1}(x_1) \wedge \mu_{B_1}(y_1) \wedge \mu_{C_1}(z_1) = 1.0 \wedge 1.0 \wedge 1.0 = 1.0.$$

The other elements of the fuzzy relation R_1 can be calculated in a similar way. The same process applies to Rule 2 and we obtain

Rule 2 — $\mu_{C_2}(z_1) = 0.2$:

	$\mu_{B_2}(y_1)$	$\mu_{B_2}(y_2)$	$\mu_{B_2}(y_3)$
	0	0.2	0.9
$\mu_{A_2}(x_1)$ 0	0	0	0
$\mu_{A_2}(x_2)$ 0.8	0	0.2	0.2
$\mu_{A_2}(x_3)$ 1.0	0	0	0.2

$\mu_{C_2}(z_2) = 0.8$:

	$\mu_{B_2}(y_1)$	$\mu_{B_2}(y_2)$	$\mu_{B_2}(y_3)$
	0	0.2	0.9
	0	0	0
	0	0.2	0.8
	0	0.2	0.8

$\mu_{C_2}(z_3) = 0.9$:

	$\mu_{B_2}(y_1)$	$\mu_{B_2}(y_2)$	$\mu_{B_2}(y_3)$
	0	0.5	0.9
	0	0	0
	0	0.2	0.8
	0	0.2	0.9

The overall fuzzy relation R is given by

$$R = R_1 \cup R_2$$

$$\text{R} = \begin{bmatrix} 1.0 & 0.5 & 0 \\ 0.6 & 0.5 & 0.2 \\ 0 & 0.2 & 0.2 \end{bmatrix} \begin{bmatrix} 0.6 & 0.5 & 0 \\ 0.6 & 0.5 & 0.8 \\ 0 & 0.2 & 0.8 \end{bmatrix} \begin{bmatrix} 0.1 & 0.1 & 0 \\ 0.1 & 0.2 & 0.8 \\ 0 & 0.2 & 0.9 \end{bmatrix}$$

For the $\wedge$ operation (logical product) in eqs. (4.10) and (4.16) we can alternatively apply algebraic product (multiplication). The details are given in Section 4.3.3.

4.3.2.b Reasoning by Fuzzy Relations and Compositional Rule of Inference

Next, I introduce the reasoning method using fuzzy relations and the compositional rule of inference.

Consider the following rules with single input and single output.

Rule 1:   IF   x is A_1 THEN   y is B_1

Rule 2:   IF   x is A_2 THEN   y is B_2.

where

x is an input variable and y is an output variable.

Let us assume we have already converted the preceding rules into fuzzy relations by the method described. For the input of fuzzy set A' on X, the output fuzzy set B' on Y can be obtained as

$$B' = A' \circ R \tag{4.18}$$

where $\circ$ denotes the composition of fuzzy relations.

Then let us consider a two-input, single-output rule such as

Rule 1   IF   x is A_1 and y is B_1 THEN   z is C_1

Rule 2   IF   x is A_1 and y is B_2 THEN   z is C_2.

where

x and y are input variables and z is an output variable.

Let us assume we have already converted the preceding rules into a fuzzy relation R. For the input of fuzzy set A' on X, and fuzzy set B' on Y, the output fuzzy set C' on Z can be obtained as

$$C' = (A' \text{ and } B') \circ R = A' \circ (B' \circ R) = B' \circ (A' \circ R). \tag{4.19}$$

When there are two variables in premises, fuzzy relation R has three terms (relation between x, y, and z). In this case we apply the two-stage composition process for reasoning as shown in (4.19).

In a similar way, we can consider n input and single-output fuzzy reasoning.

Rule 1   IF   x is A_{11} and ... and x is A_{n1}

THEN   z is C_1;

Rule 2   IF   x is A_{12} and ... and y is A_{n2}

THEN   z is C_2.

Because there are n variables in the premises, R is an $(n + 1)$-term fuzzy relation. The conclusion of reasoning C′ can be obtained as

$$C' = (A_1' \text{ and } \cdots A_n') \circ R = A_1' \circ \cdots A_n' \circ R. \tag{4.20}$$

For the general $(n + 1)$-term fuzzy relations we can obtain the conclusion by the n-stage composition process.

Composition process is detailed in Section 3.5. Let us see an example of composition in Example 4.3.

EXAMPLE 4.3. COMPOSITIONAL RULE OF INFERENCE

Let us execute fuzzy reasoning by the compositional rule of inference using the fuzzy relations in Example 4.2.

Case 1

For the two-dimensional fuzzy relation R composed by Mamdani's method, we assume an input fuzzy set A′ on X such as

$$A' = 0.8/x_1 + 0.3/x_2.$$

The conclusion of the reasoning B′ on Y will be given such as

$$B' = (A' \circ R)$$

$$= \begin{bmatrix} x_1 & x_2 & x_3 \\ 0.8 & 0.3 & 0 \end{bmatrix} \circ \begin{array}{c} \\ x_1 \\ x_2 \\ x_3 \end{array} \begin{bmatrix} y_1 & y_2 & y_3 \\ 1.0 & 0.6 & 0.1 \\ 0.6 & 0.8 & 0.8 \\ 0.2 & 0.8 & 0.9 \end{bmatrix}$$

$$= [(0.8 \wedge 1.0) \vee (0.3 \wedge 0.6) \vee (0 \wedge 0.2),$$

$$(0.8 \wedge 0.6) \vee (0.3 \wedge 0.8) \vee (0 \wedge 0.8),$$

$$(0.8 \wedge 0.1) \vee (0.3 \wedge 0.8) \vee (0 \wedge 0.9)]$$

$$= \begin{bmatrix} 0.8 \vee 0.3 \vee 0 & 0.6 \vee 0.3 \vee 0 & 0.1 \vee 0.3 \vee 0 \end{bmatrix}$$

$$= \begin{bmatrix} y_1 & y_2 & y_3 \\ 0.8 & 0.6 & 0.3 \end{bmatrix}.$$

Case 2

Next let us consider the three-dimensional fuzzy relations R by Mamdani's conversion method. If we consider input as fuzzy set A′ on X and B′ on Y. The conclusion C′ is a fuzzy set on Z and is given as

$$C' = B' \circ (A' \circ R).$$

If we write this calculation by membership functions, it will be

$$\mu_{C'1}(x, y) = \max_y \left\{ \mu_{B'}(y) \wedge \max_x[\mu_{A'}(x) \wedge \mu_R(x, y, z)] \right\}. \tag{4.21}$$

Now let us assume fuzzy sets A′ and B′ as

$$A' = 0.8/x_1 + 0.3/x_2$$
$$B' = 0.4/y_1 + 0.9/y_3.$$

Here let us define

$$\mu_T(y, z) = \max_x \left\{ \mu_{A'}(x) \vee \mu_R(x, y, z) \right\}.$$

If we notice that the preceding equation means that

$$T = A' \circ R,$$
$$C' = B' \circ (A \circ R)$$

can be rewritten as

$$C' = B' \circ T.$$

Then let us calculate T first.

$$T = A' \circ R$$

$$= \begin{array}{c} \\ y_1 \\ y_2 \\ y_3 \end{array} \begin{array}{ccc} z_1 & z_2 & z_3 \\ \left[\begin{array}{ccc} 0.8 & 0.6 & 0.1 \\ 0.5 & 0.5 & 0.2 \\ 0.2 & 0.3 & 0.3 \end{array}\right]. \end{array}$$

Next, calculate C:

$$C' = B' \circ T$$

$$= \begin{array}{ccc} y_1 & y_2 & y_3 \\ [0, & 0.4 & 0.9] \end{array} \circ \begin{array}{c} y_1 \\ y_2 \\ y_3 \end{array} \begin{array}{ccc} z_1 & z_2 & z_3 \\ \left[\begin{array}{ccc} 0.8 & 0.6 & 0.1 \\ 0.5 & 0.5 & 0.2 \\ 0.2 & 0.3 & 0.3 \end{array}\right] \end{array}$$

$$= \begin{array}{ccc} z_1 & z_2 & z_3 \\ [0.4 & 0.4, & 0.3] \end{array}$$

4.3.3 Fuzzy Reasoning Using Various Implications

In the previous section, I have shown the methods of composing fuzzy relations proposed by Zadeh and Mamdani. In this section, the method of composing fuzzy relations by various other methods is described. The representing implication formulae for fuzzy reasoning are shown in Table 4.3.1.

For Mamdani's implication $a \rightarrow b = a \wedge b$ we can use algebraic product (multiplication), bounded product, or drastic product instead. These operations satisfy the same condition known as T-norm.

TABLE 4.3.1.   Various implications.

1	Mamdani's method (Logical product)	$a \rightarrow b = a \wedge b$
2	algebraic product	$a \rightarrow b = a \cdot b$
3	bounded product	$a \rightarrow b = 0 \vee (a + b - 1)$
4	drastic product	$a \rightarrow b = \begin{cases} a & \text{as } b = 1 \\ b & \text{as } a = 1 \\ 0 & \text{otherwise} \end{cases}$
5	Zadeh's method (Lukasiewicz's implication)	$a \rightarrow b = 1 \wedge (1 - a + b)$
6	Boolean logic implication	$a \rightarrow b = (1 - a) \vee b$
7	Goedel logic implication	$a \rightarrow b = \begin{cases} 1 & a \le b \\ b & a > b \end{cases}$
8	Goguen's implication	$a \rightarrow b = \begin{cases} 1 & a \le b \\ b/a & a > b \end{cases}$

Implications 1–4 use $\vee$-operation to aggregate the individual conclusions from each rule as in Mamdani's method (4.17). On the other hand, implications 5–8 use $\wedge$-operation as in Zadeh's method.

Table 4.3.1 shows there are variations of methods for constructing fuzzy relations other than Mamdani's and Zadeh's methods. However, in any implication we can still apply the composition process shown in Section 4.3.2 for a conclusion based on the fuzzy relations.

EXAMPLE 4.4. COMPOSITION OF FUZZY RELATIONS BY VARIOUS IMPLICATIONS

Mamdani's conversion method and Zadeh's method shown in Example 4.3 are based on implications 1 and 5, respectively, in Table 4.3.1. However, various other fuzzy relations can be composed using different interpretations of the implication. In this example, we try to convert the rules given in Example 4.3 using other methods.

In Example 4.2 we considered the rules:

Rule 1:   IF x is A_1 THEN y is B_1

Rule 2:   IF x is A_2 THEN y is B_2

where

$X = \{x_1, x_2, x_3\}$ and $A_1, A_2 \subset X$

$Y = \{y_1, y_2, y_3\}$ and $B_1, B_2 \subset Y$.

Fuzzy sets $A_1, A_2, B_1,$ and B_2 are given as

$A_1 = 1.0/x_1 + 0.6/x_2$

$A_2 = 0.8/x_2 + 1.0/x_3$

$B_1 = 1.0/y_1 + 0.6/y_2 + 0.1/y_3$

$B_2 = 0.2/y_1 + 0.8/y_2 + 0.9/y_3$

(i) Implication 2

$$
R_1 = \begin{array}{c} \\ \mu_{A_1}(x_1) \\ \mu_{A_1}(x_2) \\ \mu_{A_1}(x_3) \end{array}
\begin{array}{c} \\ 1.0 \\ 0.6 \\ 0 \end{array}
\begin{array}{c} \mu_{B_1}(y_1) \quad \mu_{B_1}(y_2) \quad \mu_{B_1}(y_3) \\ 1.0 \qquad\quad 0.6 \qquad\quad 0.1 \\ \left[\begin{array}{ccc} 1.0 & 0.6 & 0.1 \\ 0.6 & 0.36 & 0.06 \\ 0 & 0 & 0 \end{array} \right] \end{array}
$$

$$
R_2 = \begin{array}{c} \\ \mu_{A_2}(x_1) \\ \mu_{A_2}(x_2) \\ \mu_{A_2}(x_3) \end{array}
\begin{array}{c} \\ 0 \\ 0.8 \\ 1.0 \end{array}
\begin{array}{c} \mu_{B_2}(y_1) \quad \mu_{B_2}(y_2) \quad \mu_{B_2}(y_3) \\ 0.2 \qquad\quad 0.8 \qquad\quad 0.9 \\ \left[\begin{array}{ccc} 0 & 0 & 0 \\ 0.16 & 0.64 & 0.72 \\ 0.2 & 0.8 & 0.9 \end{array} \right] \end{array}.
$$

The overall fuzzy relation R is given by Mamdani's formula of (4.17a) as

$$R = R_1 \cup R_2 = \begin{bmatrix} 1.0 & 0.6 & 0.1 \\ 0.6 & 0.64 & 0.72 \\ 0.2 & 0.8 & 0.9 \end{bmatrix}.$$

(ii) Implication 3

$$R_1 = \begin{array}{c} \\ \mu_{A_1}(x_1) \quad 1.0 \\ \mu_{A_1}(x_2) \quad 0.6 \\ \mu_{A_1}(x_3) \quad 0 \end{array} \begin{array}{ccc} \mu_{B_1}(y_1) & \mu_{B_1}(y_2) & \mu_{B_1}(y_3) \\ 1.0 & 0.6 & 0.1 \\ \begin{bmatrix} 1.0 & 0.6 & 0.1 \\ 0.6 & 0.2 & 0 \\ 0 & 0 & 0 \end{bmatrix} \end{array}$$

$$R_2 = \begin{array}{c} \\ \mu_{A_2}(x_1) \quad 0 \\ \mu_{A_2}(x_2) \quad 0.8 \\ \mu_{A_2}(x_3) \quad 1.0 \end{array} \begin{array}{ccc} \mu_{B_2}(y_1) & \mu_{B_2}(y_2) & \mu_{B_2}(y_3) \\ 0.2 & 0.8 & 0.9 \\ \begin{bmatrix} 0 & 0 & 0 \\ 0 & 0.6 & 0.7 \\ 0.2 & 0.8 & 0.9 \end{bmatrix} \end{array}.$$

The overall fuzzy relation R is given by Mamdani's formula of (4.17a) as

$$R = R_1 \cup R_2 = \begin{bmatrix} 1.0 & 0.6 & 0 \\ 0.6 & 0.6 & 0.7 \\ 0.2 & 0.8 & 0.9 \end{bmatrix}.$$

(iii) Implication 4

$$R_1 = \begin{array}{c} \\ \mu_{A_1}(x_1) \quad 1.0 \\ \mu_{A_1}(x_2) \quad 0.6 \\ \mu_{A_1}(x_3) \quad 0 \end{array} \begin{array}{ccc} \mu_{B_1}(y_1) & \mu_{B_1}(y_2) & \mu_{B_1}(y_3) \\ 1.0 & 0.6 & 0.1 \\ \begin{bmatrix} 1.0 & 0.6 & 0.1 \\ 0.6 & 0 & 0 \\ 0 & 0 & 0 \end{bmatrix} \end{array}$$

$$R_2 = \begin{array}{c} \\ \mu_{A_2}(x_1) \quad 0 \\ \mu_{A_2}(x_2) \quad 0.8 \\ \mu_{A_2}(x_3) \quad 1.0 \end{array} \begin{array}{ccc} \mu_{B_2}(y_1) & \mu_{B_2}(y_2) & \mu_{B_2}(y_3) \\ 0.2 & 0.8 & 0.9 \\ \begin{bmatrix} 0 & 0 & 0 \\ 0 & 0 & 0 \\ 0.2 & 0.8 & 0.9 \end{bmatrix} \end{array}.$$

The overall fuzzy relation R is given by Mamdani's formula of (4.17a) as

$$R = R_1 \cup R_2 = \begin{bmatrix} 1.0 & 0.6 & 0.1 \\ 0.6 & 0 & 0 \\ 0.2 & 0.8 & 0.9 \end{bmatrix}.$$

(iv) Implication 6

$$
\begin{array}{c}
\begin{array}{ccc} \mu_{B_1}(y_1) & \mu_{B_1}(y_2) & \mu_{B_1}(y_3) \\ 1.0 & 0.6 & 0.1 \end{array} \\
R_1 = \begin{array}{cc} \mu_{A_1}(x_1) & 1.0 \\ \mu_{A_1}(x_2) & 0.6 \\ \mu_{A_1}(x_3) & 0 \end{array} \left[\begin{array}{ccc} 1.0 & 0.6 & 0.1 \\ 1.0 & 0.6 & 0.4 \\ 1.0 & 1.0 & 1.0 \end{array} \right]
\end{array}
$$

$$
\begin{array}{c}
\begin{array}{ccc} \mu_{B_2}(y_1) & \mu_{B_2}(y_2) & \mu_{B_2}(y_3) \\ 0.2 & 0.8 & 0.9 \end{array} \\
R_2 = \begin{array}{cc} \mu_{A_2}(x_1) & 0 \\ \mu_{A_2}(x_2) & 0.8 \\ \mu_{A_2}(x_3) & 1.0 \end{array} \left[\begin{array}{ccc} 1.0 & 1.0 & 1.0 \\ 0.2 & 0.8 & 0.9 \\ 0.2 & 0.8 & 0.9 \end{array} \right].
\end{array}
$$

The overall fuzzy relation R is given by Zadeh's formula of (4.17b) as

$$
R = R_1 \cap R_2 = \begin{bmatrix} 1.0 & 0.6 & 0.1 \\ 0.2 & 0.6 & 0.4 \\ 0.2 & 0.8 & 0.9 \end{bmatrix}.
$$

(v) Implication 7

$$
\begin{array}{c}
\begin{array}{ccc} \mu_{B_1}(y_1) & \mu_{B_1}(y_2) & \mu_{B_1}(y_3) \\ 1.0 & 0.6 & 0.1 \end{array} \\
R_1 = \begin{array}{cc} \mu_{A_1}(x_1) & 1.0 \\ \mu_{A_1}(x_2) & 0.6 \\ \mu_{A_1}(x_3) & 0 \end{array} \left[\begin{array}{ccc} 1.0 & 0.6 & 0.1 \\ 1.0 & 1.0 & 0.1 \\ 1.0 & 1.0 & 1.0 \end{array} \right]
\end{array}
$$

$$
\begin{array}{c}
\begin{array}{ccc} \mu_{B_2}(y_1) & \mu_{B_2}(y_2) & \mu_{B_2}(y_3) \\ 0.2 & 0.8 & 0.9 \end{array} \\
R_2 = \begin{array}{cc} \mu_{A_2}(x_1) & 0 \\ \mu_{A_2}(x_2) & 0.8 \\ \mu_{A_2}(x_3) & 1.0 \end{array} \left[\begin{array}{ccc} 1.0 & 1.0 & 1.0 \\ 0.2 & 1.0 & 1.0 \\ 0.2 & 0.8 & 0.9 \end{array} \right].
\end{array}
$$

The overall fuzzy relation R is given by Zadeh's formula of (4.17b) as

$$
R = R_1 \cap R_2 = \begin{bmatrix} 1.0 & 0.6 & 0.1 \\ 0.2 & 1.0 & 0.4 \\ 0.2 & 0.8 & 0.9 \end{bmatrix}.
$$

(vi) Implication 8

$$
R_1 = \begin{matrix} & & \mu_{B_1}(y_1) & \mu_{B_1}(y_2) & \mu_{B_1}(y_3) \\ & & 1.0 & 0.6 & 0.1 \\ \mu_{A_1}(x_1) & 1.0 \\ \mu_{A_1}(x_2) & 0.6 \\ \mu_{A_1}(x_3) & 0 \end{matrix} \begin{bmatrix} 1.0 & 0.6 & 0.1 \\ 1.0 & 1.0 & 0.17 \\ 1.0 & 1.0 & 1.0 \end{bmatrix}
$$

$$
R_2 = \begin{matrix} & & \mu_{B_2}(y_1) & \mu_{B_2}(y_2) & \mu_{B_2}(y_3) \\ & & 0.2 & 0.8 & 0.9 \\ \mu_{A_2}(x_1) & 0 \\ \mu_{A_2}(x_2) & 0.8 \\ \mu_{A_2}(x_3) & 0.1 \end{matrix} \begin{bmatrix} 1.0 & 1.0 & 1.0 \\ 0.25 & 1.0 & 1.0 \\ 0.2 & 0.8 & 0.9 \end{bmatrix} .
$$

The overall fuzzy relation R is given by Zadeh's formula of (4.17b) as

$$
R = R_1 \cap R_2 = \begin{bmatrix} 1.0 & 0.6 & 0.1 \\ 0.25 & 1.0 & 0.17 \\ 0.2 & 0.8 & 0.9 \end{bmatrix} .
$$

4.4 Method 2: Fuzzy Reasoning Using Linear Functions

When there are many variables in premises, the direct method of fuzzy reasoning has the following difficulties.

1. The number of rules increases exponentially with the number of premise-part variables;
2. as the number of rules increases, the labor of constructing rules becomes excessively burdensome;
3. if the number of premise-part variables becomes too large, it becomes generally difficult to grasp the causal relationship between the premises and consequences, and eventually too difficult to construct rules.

To solve these problems, a fuzzy reasoning mechanism was devised using linear functions for the consequence part. This reasoning method has the following features.

1. The consequence part of the rule uses linear input-output functions;
2. we can identify rules by modeling based on input-output data.

This modeling method was proposed by Takagi, Kang, and Sugeno [2;3;4]. Because of the modeling, the construction of rules is not a manual procedure, thus it solves Problems 2 and 3 of the direct method. Problem 1 can be also handled with this method and I show this in Example 4.5. For practical application of this method, we need a modeling approach using input-output data. However, because we need much knowledge, for example, on system identification, to fully understand the modeling procedure, the modeling itself is beyond the scope of this book.

The situation of many premise-part variables implies that the problem of reasoning is complicated. For example, let us consider an operation procedure observing the thermometer of a certain piece of equipment and adjusting the switch of a heater. If there are two thermometers, A and B, the causal relationship of the thermometers and the heater will be simply expressed by a logical form such as "IF thermometer A is 'Low' and thermometer B is 'Quite Low,' THEN raise the switch level for the heater to 'Rather High.'"

On the other hand, if there are 10 thermometers, namely, A, B, C, D, E, F, G, H, I, and J, it is difficult to express the operation procedure in a logical form such as "IF thermometer A and E are 'Slightly Low' AND B and H are 'Quite High' AND C, I, and J are 'Moderate' AND D is 'Slightly High' AND F is 'Quite Low' AND G is 'High,' THEN a proper level of the switch for a heater is. . .." Experienced human operators can determine the switch level almost immediately after watching the thermometers, but it is hard to construct matching rules for their operation procedures. However, we can still record the thermometer readings and the corresponding operator actions. Using these input-output data we can perform modeling and construct reasoning rules in the fuzzy reasoning method explained in the following.

Although I pointed out some problems of the direct method of fuzzy reasoning, it is not necessarily inferior to the fuzzy reasoning method using linear equations in the consequence part. The latter method assumes modeling, which requires input-output data, and the modeling process is not easy to perform. In general, for the reasoning object with a small number of premise-part variables, the direct method is preferable.

Fuzzy reasoning method using linear functions in the consequence part

In this reasoning method, we use the following rules

Rule i   IF x_1 is A^i1 and ... and x1 is A^in

THEN $y^i = c_0^i + c_1^i + \cdots + c_n^i x_n$,

i = 1, 2, . . . , r   (4.22)

where i is the suffix of rules, r is the total number of rules, and A_{ik} (k = 1, 2, . . . , n) are fuzzy sets. x_k is an input variable, y_i is the output from the ith rule, and c_{ik} is the parameter of the consequence in the ith rule.

Fuzzy reasoning value is given by the weighted mean:

$$y = \left(\sum_{i=1}^{l} w^i y^i \right) \Big/ \sum_{i=1}^{l} w^i$$ (4.23)

where w^i is the adaptability of the premises of the ith rule and given by the equation:

$$w^i = \prod_{k=1}^{n} \mu_{A_k^i(x_k)}$$

(4.24)

where $\mu_{A_k^i}(x_k)$ is the membership value of the fuzzy set A_{ik}.

Because this reasoning method uses linear functions in the consequence part, it can express the same input-output relations as the direct method with a smaller number of rules. The next example shows the comparison of the number of rules between this method and the direct method.

EXAMPLE 4.5. COMPARISON WITH DIRECT METHOD

Suppose the following are the rules for the direct method.

IF   x is "Small" and y is "Small"   THEN   z is "Medium"

IF   x is "Small" and y is "Medium"   THEN   z is "Small"

IF   x is "Small" and y is "Big"   THEN   z is "Very Small"

IF   x is "Medium" and y is "Small"   THEN   z is "Big"

IF   x is "Medium" and y is "Medium"   THEN   z is "Medium"

IF   x is "Medium" and y is "Big"   THEN   z is "Small"

IF   x is "Big" and y is "Small"   THEN   z is "Very Big"

IF   x is "Big" and y is "Medium"   THEN   z is "Medium"

IF   x is "Big" and y is "Big"   THEN   z is "Very Small"

The fuzzy sets used in the preceding rules are shown in Figure 4.9.
If we replace these fuzzy sets with practical fuzzy numbers such as

Very Big   = about 10,

Big   = about 8,

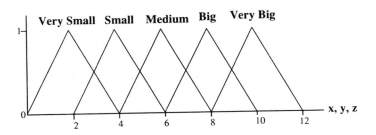

FIGURE 4.9. Fuzzy sets for consequence part.

Medium   = about 6,

Small   = about 4,

Very Small   = about 2,

we can rewrite the preceding rules as follows.

IF   x is "about 4" and y is "about 4"   THEN   z is "about 6"

IF   x is "about 4" and y is "about 6"   THEN   z is "about 4"

IF   x is "about 4" and y is "about 8"   THEN   z is "about 2"

IF   x is "about 6" and y is "about 4"   THEN   z is "about 8"

IF   x is "about 6" and y is "about 6"   THEN   z is "about 6"

IF   x is "about 6" and y is "about 8"   THEN   z is "about 4"

IF   x is "about 8" and y is "about 4"   THEN   z is "about 10"

IF   x is "about 8" and y is "about 6"   THEN   z is "about 6"

IF   x is "about 8" and y is "about 8"   THEN   z is "about 2"

For simplicity we replace the fuzzy numbers with definite numbers such as

IF   x is 4 and y is 4   THEN   z is 6

IF   x is 4 and y is 6   THEN   z is 4

IF   x is 4 and y is 8   THEN   z is 2

IF   x is 6 and y is 4   THEN   z is 8

IF   x is 6 and y is 6   THEN   z is 6

IF   x is 6 and y is 8   THEN   z is 4

IF   x is 8 and y is 4   THEN   z is 10

IF   x is 8 and y is 6   THEN   z is 6

IF   x is 8 and y is 8   THEN   z is 2

Figure 4.10 shows the input-output relations of the simplified model on the X–Y plane.

The input-output relation can be expressed by two linear equations. If we use the format of (4.22), it becomes

IF   x is "Big"   THEN $z=-2y+18$

IF   y is "Small or Medium"   THEN $z=x-y+6$.

The original number of rules was nine but it has now been reduced to two. Although this example is intentional, the tendency is apparent as the number of variables increases.

EXAMPLE 4.6. DESCRIPTION OF REASONING USING LINEAR EQUATIONS

Figure 4.11 shows a nonlinear relationship between x and y. If we are to approximate with a linear equation, we cannot expect good accuracy. However, we

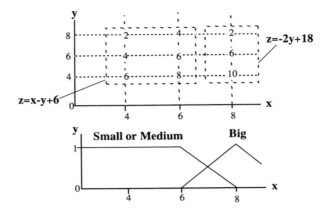

FIGURE 4.10. Input-output relationship of simplified fuzzy model.

can express such a nonlinear relationship using the fuzzy reasoning rule format
such as

IF   y is "Small"   THEN   y=0.5 x+2.0
IF   x is "Big"   THEN   y=0.2 x+6.0.

For $1 < x < 2$, the adaptability figures of both preceding rules are more than
0, and the reasoning output shows nonlinearity as depicted by the broken line in
Figure 4.11. This is due to the weighted mean of the adaptability.

This method of fuzzy reasoning can express the behavior of complex systems by
a small number of rules. It has proved to be effective in multiple-variable, nonlinear
system applications such as the estimation of river inflow and the modeling and
control of multilayer sludge incinerators [3].

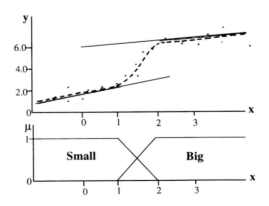

FIGURE 4.11. Nonlinear input-output relation.

4.5 Method 3: Simplified Fuzzy Reasoning

Simplified Fuzzy Reasoning We can consider that the fuzzy reasoning method with simplified consequence part is a special case of the direct method or the method using linear functions. If we replace the fuzzy sets in the consequence part with a singleton (real value), we obtain the simplified method. Alternatively, we can leave the constant term only and omit the higher term in the linear functions of Method 2, and we also get the simplified method.

Fuzzy reasoning method with simplified consequence part

A two-input, one-output fuzzy reasoning rule is expressed as

Rule i   IF x_1 is A^i and   y is B^i

        THEN $z = c^i$,

        $i = 1, 2, \ldots, r$ (4.25)

where i is the suffix of rules, r is the total number of rules, A_i, B_i are fuzzy sets, and c is a real value constant.

The conclusion of the reasoning is given by

$$z = \frac{\sum_{i=1}^{r} w^i z^i}{\sum_{i=1}^{r} w^i} = \frac{\sum_{i=1}^{r} w^i c^i}{\sum_{i=1}^{r} w^i} \qquad (4.26)$$

where w_i is the adaptability of the premise part of Rule i and calculated by

$w^i = \mu_{A^i}(x) \wedge \mu_{B^i}(y)$.

The simplified method has the following advantages over the direct method.

1. The reasoning mechanism is simple;
2. the computation is fast; and
3. the results are hardly different from those of the direct method.

Because the practical merits have been recognized, the simplified methods have been applied more often than the original direct method.

4.6 Application Example of Fuzzy Reasoning

For an application example of fuzzy reasoning we again look into the driving logic (speed control of a car) described in Example 4.1. In this example, we particularly try the following procedures:

a. to convert fuzzy IF-THEN rules into fuzzy relations; and
b. to execute fuzzy reasoning by applying the compositional rule of inference to the fuzzy relations obtained previously.

The linguistic driving rules are repeated for the reader's convenience.

Rule 1:   IF   distance between cars is short

           AND   speed is slow,

           THEN   hold the gas pedal steady (maintain the speed).

Rule 2:   IF   distance between cars is short

           AND   speed is fast,

           THEN   step on the brake (reduce the speed).

Rule 3:   IF   distance between cars is long

           AND   speed is slow,

           THEN   step on the gas pedal (increase the speed).

Rule 4:   IF   distance between cars is long

           AND   speed is fast,

           THEN   hold the gas pedal steady (maintain the speed).

4.6.1 Step 1: Composition of fuzzy relations

In Example 4.1, the fuzzy IF-THEN rules are written as follows.

Rule 1   IF   x is A_1 and y is B_1 THEN   z is C_1

Rule 2   IF   x is A_1 and y is B_2 THEN   z is C_2

Rule 3   IF   x is A_2 and y is B_1 THEN   z is C_3

Rule 4   IF   x is A_2 and y is B_2 THEN   z is C_1

Here we assume the set of distances between cars (m) such as

$$X = \{x_1, x_2, x_3\} = \{10, 20, 30\}$$

and the set of speeds (km/h) such as

$$Y = \{y_1, y_2, y_3\} = \{30, 50, 70\}.$$

Also, the accelerations (km/h^2) as

$$Z = \{z_1, z_2, z_3\} = \{-10, 0, 10\}.$$

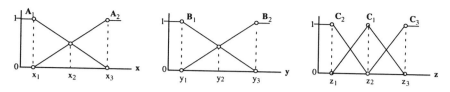

FIGURE 4.12. Fuzzy sets for driving logic

The fuzzy sets used in the preceding four rules can be quantized as in the Figure 4.12.

$$A_1 = \begin{bmatrix} 1.0 & 0.5 & 0 \end{bmatrix} \quad B_1 = \begin{bmatrix} 10 & 0.5 & 0 \end{bmatrix} \quad C_1 = \begin{bmatrix} 0 & 1.0 & 0 \end{bmatrix}$$
$$A_2 = \begin{bmatrix} 0 & 0.5 & 1.0 \end{bmatrix} \quad B_2 = \begin{bmatrix} 0 & 0.5 & 10 \end{bmatrix} \quad C_2 = \begin{bmatrix} 1.0 & 0 & 0 \end{bmatrix}$$
$$C_3 = \begin{bmatrix} 0 & 0 & 1.0 \end{bmatrix}$$

Here, note that the number of elements in X, Y, Z is three and fuzzy sets A, B, C, are also quantized into three elements.

In ordinary cases we quantize these parameters into more elements. As the number of elements is small, the approximation becomes more rough. In this example, I use a particularly small number of elements to aid the reader's comprehension.

As shown in Section 4.3.2, we compose one fuzzy relation for one corresponding fuzzy IF-THEN rule. Now let us construct fuzzy relations by Mamdani's conversion method. Because there are three elements, x, y, and z, the conversion formula becomes:

$$\mu_R(x_i, y_j, z_k) = \mu_A(x_i) \wedge \mu_B(y_j) \wedge \mu_C(z_k)$$
$$i, j, k = 1, 2, 3.$$

By the preceding conversion formula we get the fuzzy relation R_1 from the first rule:

$$R_1 = \begin{array}{c}\\ \mu_{A_1}(x_1)\ 1.0 \\ \mu_{A_1}(x_2)\ 0.5 \\ \mu_{A_1}(x_3)\ 0 \end{array}
\begin{array}{ccc}
\mu_{B_1}(y_1) & \mu_{B_1}(y_2) & \mu_{B_1}(y_3) \\
1.0 & 0.5 & 0 \\
\hline
0 & 0 & 0 \\
0 & 0 & 0 \\
0 & 0 & 0 \\
\hline
\multicolumn{3}{c}{0} \\
\multicolumn{3}{c}{\mu_{C_1}(z_1)}
\end{array}$$

$$\begin{array}{ccc}
\mu_{B_1}(y_1) & \mu_{B_1}(y_2) & \mu_{B_1}(y_3) \\
1.0 & 0.5 & 0 \\
\hline
1.0 & 0.5 & 0 \\
1.0 & 0.5 & 0 \\
0.5 & 0.5 & 0 \\
0 & 0 & 0 \\
\hline
\multicolumn{3}{c}{1.0} \\
\multicolumn{3}{c}{\mu_{C_1}(z_2)}
\end{array}$$

$$\begin{array}{ccc}
\mu_{B_1}(y_1) & \mu_{B_1}(y_2) & \mu_{B_1}(y_3) \\
1.0 & 0.5 & 0 \\
\hline
1.0 & 0.5 & 0 \\
0 & 0 & 0 \\
0 & 0 & 0 \\
\hline
\multicolumn{3}{c}{0} \\
\multicolumn{3}{c}{\mu_{C_1}(z_3)}
\end{array}$$

Here the shaded element is given by the formula as

$$\mu_{R_1}(x_1, y_1, z_1) = \mu_{A_1}(x_1) \wedge \mu_{B_1}(y_1) \wedge \mu_{C_1}(z_1)$$
$$= 1.0 \wedge 1.0 \wedge 0 = 0.$$

The other elements are obtained similarly.

Let us convert Rules 2, 3, and 4 into fuzzy relations R_2, R_3, and R_4, accordingly.

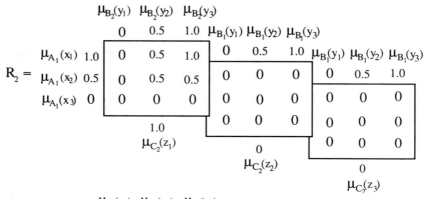

$R_2 = $

	$\mu_{B_2}(y_1)$ 0	$\mu_{B_2}(y_2)$ 0.5	$\mu_{B_2}(y_3)$ 1.0
$\mu_{A_1}(x_1)$ 1.0	0	0.5	1.0
$\mu_{A_1}(x_2)$ 0.5	0	0.5	0.5
$\mu_{A_1}(x_3)$ 0	0	0	0

$\mu_{C_2}(z_1)$ = 1.0

	$\mu_{B_1}(y_1)$ 0	$\mu_{B_1}(y_2)$ 0.5	$\mu_{B_1}(y_3)$ 1.0
	0	0	0
	0	0	0
	0	0	0

$\mu_{C_2}(z_2)$ = 0

	$\mu_{B_1}(y_1)$ 0	$\mu_{B_1}(y_2)$ 0.5	$\mu_{B_1}(y_3)$ 1.0
	0	0.5	1.0
	0	0	0
	0	0	0
	0	0	0

$\mu_{C_2}(z_3)$ = 0

$R_3 = $

	$\mu_{B_1}(y_1)$ 1.0	$\mu_{B_1}(y_2)$ 0.5	$\mu_{B_1}(y_3)$ 0
$\mu_{A_2}(x_1)$ 0	0	0	0
$\mu_{A_2}(x_2)$ 0.5	0	0	0
$\mu_{A_2}(x_3)$ 1.0	0	0	0

$\mu_{C_3}(z_1)$ = 0

	$\mu_{B_1}(y_1)$ 1.0	$\mu_{B_1}(y_2)$ 0.5	$\mu_{B_1}(y_3)$ 0
	1.0	0.5	0
	0	0	0
	0	0	0

$\mu_{C_3}(z_2)$ = 0

	$\mu_{B_1}(y_1)$ 1.0	$\mu_{B_1}(y_2)$ 0.5	$\mu_{B_1}(y_3)$ 0
	1.0	0.5	0
	0	0	0
	0.5	0.5	0
	1.0	0.5	0

$\mu_{C_3}(z_3)$ = 1.0

$R_4 = $

	$\mu_{B_2}(y_1)$ 0	$\mu_{B_2}(y_2)$ 0.5	$\mu_{B_2}(y_3)$ 1.0
$\mu_{A_2}(x_1)$ 0	0	0	0
$\mu_{A_2}(x_2)$ 0.5	0	0	0
$\mu_{A_2}(x_3)$ 1.0	0	0	0

$\mu_{C_1}(z_1)$ = 0

	$\mu_{B_2}(y_1)$ 0	$\mu_{B_2}(y_2)$ 0.5	$\mu_{B_2}(y_3)$ 1.0
	0	0	0
	0	0.5	0.5
	0	0.5	1.0

$\mu_{C_1}(z_2)$ = 1.0

	$\mu_{B_2}(y_1)$ 0	$\mu_{B_2}(y_2)$ 0.5	$\mu_{B_2}(y_3)$ 1.0
	0	0.5	1.0
	0	0	0
	0	0	0
	0	0	0

$\mu_{C_1}(z_3)$ = 0

The total fuzzy relation R is given by

$$R = R_1 \cup R_2 \cup R_3 \cup R_4$$

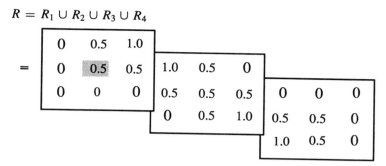

Here the shaded element is given by the formula as

$$\mu_R(x_2, y_2, z_1) = \bigvee_{h=1}^{4} \mu_{R_h}(x_2, y_2, z_1) = 0 \vee 0.5 \vee 0 \vee 0 = 0.5.$$

4.6.2 Step 2: Reasoning by Fuzzy Relations and Compositional Rule

Let us now realize fuzzy reasoning by the fuzzy relations composed in Section 4.6.1. For fuzzy reasoning, we apply the compositional rule of inference introduced in Section 4.3.2.

Suppose the distance between the cars is 10 m and the speed is 30 km/h. Such a situation can be described by fuzzy sets A′ and B′ as

distance (m) $A' = \begin{matrix} 10 & 20 & 30 \\ [1.0 & 0 & 0\,] \end{matrix}$

speed (km/h) $B' = \begin{matrix} 30 & 50 & 70 \\ [1.0 & 0 & 0\,]. \end{matrix}$

Let us compute the conclusion of the reasoning then. Suppose C′ is the fuzzy set that represents the conclusion, and C′ can be calculated by

$$C' = (A' \text{ and } B') \circ R$$
$$= A' \circ (B' \circ R)$$
$$= B' \circ (A' \circ R)$$

where ∘ stands for the composition process.

In the calculation of B′ ∘ (A′ ∘ R), let us first calculate the term A′ ∘ R and represent it with T. T is then given as

$$T = A' \circ R$$

$$
\begin{array}{ccc} x_1 & x_2 & x_3 \\ = [\,1.0 & 0 & 0\,] \end{array} \circ
\begin{array}{c|ccc} & y_1 & y_2 & y_3 \\ \hline x_1 & 0 & 0.5 & 1.0 \\ x_2 & 0 & 0.5 & 0.5 \\ x_3 & 0 & 0 & 0 \end{array}
\begin{array}{c|ccc} & y_1 & y_2 & y_3 \\ \hline & 1.0 & 0.5 & 0 \\ & 0.5 & 0.5 & 0.5 \\ & 0 & 0.5 & 1.0 \\ z_1 \end{array}
\begin{array}{c|ccc} & y_1 & y_2 & y_3 \\ \hline & 0 & 0 & 0 \\ & 0.5 & 0.5 & 0 \\ & 1.0 & 0.5 & 0 \\ z_2 \end{array}
\begin{array}{ccc} z_3 \end{array}
$$

$$
= \begin{array}{c|ccc} & z_1 & z_2 & z_3 \\ \hline y_1 & 0 & 1.0 & 0 \\ y_2 & 0.5 & 0.5 & 0 \\ y_3 & 1.0 & 0 & 0 \end{array}.
$$

The overall conclusion C' is now calculated by

$$C' = B' \circ T$$

$$
= \begin{array}{ccc} y_1 & y_2 & y_3 \\ [\,1.0 & 0 & 0\,] \end{array} \circ
\begin{array}{c|ccc} & z_1 & z_2 & z_3 \\ \hline y_1 & 0 & 1.0 & 0 \\ y_2 & 0.5 & 0.5 & 0 \\ y_3 & 1.0 & 0 & 0 \end{array}
$$

$$
= \begin{array}{ccc} z_1 & z_2 & z_3 \\ [\,0 & 1.0 & 0\,]. \end{array}
$$

Here C' is a fuzzy set. When we defuzzify C' by taking its center of gravity with the weighted mean, we get a definite value:

$$\frac{0 \times z_1 + 1.0 \times z_2 + 0 \times z_3}{0 + 1.0 + 0}.$$

Note that the accelerations are $z_1 = -10 \text{ km/h}^2$, $z_2 = 0 \text{ km/h}^2$, and $z_3 = 10 \text{ km/h}^2$. We get the definite value of

$$\frac{0 \times (-10) + 1.0 \times 0 + 0 \times 10}{0 + 1.0 + 0} = 0.$$

Inasmuch as z is the required speed adjustment (acceleration), this result, for the distance of 10 m and the speed of 30 km/h, can be interpreted as "keep the present speed."

The reasoning process described is when the distance between the cars is 10 m and the speed is 30 km/h. Other possible options for the input include 20 or 30 m for the distance and 50 or 70 km/h for speed. If we think of all possible combinations, there are eight combinations ($2^3 = 8$). All the possible options are summarized in

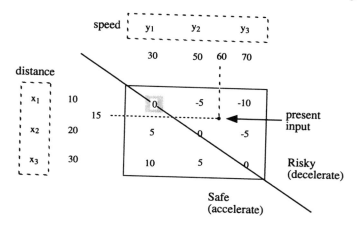

FIGURE 4.13. Fuzzy reasoning for driving a car.

Figure 4.13. The numbers in the figure indicate the conclusions (speed adjustment). This figure gives us the following perspective: to keep a constant speed, when the speed is slow the distance can be short, but the distance should be long when the speed is high. This is consistent with what linguistic rules Rules 1 and 4 indicate. We also notice that when the speed goes to risky (high speed), there is a deceleration conclusion deduced, and when the speed goes to safe (low speed), an acceleration is inferred. This is consistent with Rules 2 and 3.

References

[1] Sugeno, M. 1985. An introductory survey on fuzzy control. *Information Sciences*, 36: 59–83.

[2] Takagi, T. and Sugeno, M. 1985. Fuzzy identification of systems and its applications to modeling and control. *IEEE Transactions on Systems, Man and Cybernetics*, 15, 1: 116–132.

[3] Sugeno, M. and Kang, G. T. 1986. Fuzzy modeling and control of multi-layer incinerator. *Fuzzy Sets and Systems*, 18: 329–346.

[4] Sugeno, M. and Kang, G.T. 1988. Structure identification of fuzzy model. *Fuzzy Sets and Systems* 28; 15–33.

[5] Mamdani, E. H. 1974. Applications of fuzzy algorithms for control of a simple dynamic plant. *Proceedings of IEEE*, 121, 12; 1585–1588.

[6] Mizumoto, M. 1988. Fuzzy controls under various fuzzy reasoning methods. *Information Sciences* 45; 129–151.

[7] Tsukamoto, Y. 1979. Fuzzy logic based on Lukasiewicz logic and its application to diagnosis and control, Ph.D. Dissertation, Tokyo Institute of Technology.

5

Fuzzy Logic Control

In the recent development of industrial systems, fuzzy logic control has been the focus of interest in applications of fuzzy set theory. In this chapter, only basic concepts of fuzzy control are given because a detailed analysis would require the readers to have knowledge of control engineering. First, a general idea of fuzzy logic control is given and the design approach of fuzzy controllers is described. Then application examples of fuzzy logic control are presented.

5.1 What is Fuzzy Logic Control?

The purpose of fuzzy logic control is, simply put, the realization of human control strategy. Control strategies in conventional controllers such as PID (Proportional-Integral-Derivative) controllers are expressed in mathematical functions. This is fundamentally different from human control. If we consider the situation of driving a car, the difference between human operation and conventional controllers is evident. The operation of gas pedal and brake is determined by the overall decision on the situation. For example, when climbing a hill, we know the car will lose speed if no action is taken. Therefore we step on the pedal for more gas when the hill is steep, and maybe only a little when it is not so steep. Furthermore, if the car loses speed even though we stepped on the gas, we would step on it for much more gas. This kind of human control strategy is difficult and unnatural to express in mathematical functions. Fuzzy logic control, on the other hand, makes use of human knowledge and experience to perform in a fashion similar to the human strategy, thus realizing an intelligent control.

For fuzzy logic control, we need to establish fuzzy IF-THEN rules. The IF-THEN rules used in fuzzy logic control are called the control rules. For the fuzzy IF-THEN rules, we often exploit the knowledge of operators who are actually involved in the operation of a target system. Once we establish the fuzzy IF-THEN rules, we can realize the control strategy by fuzzy reasoning. The structure of the fuzzy logic controller is thus the structure of fuzzy reasoning itself. The three methods of fuzzy reasoning, introduced in Chapter 4, can be applied to make three different types of fuzzy controllers. In this chapter, I describe only the application of the direct method because: (a) there is little difference between the direct method and the simplified method; and (b) the reasoning method that uses linear functions for the consequence part assumes a modeling approach to establish IF-THEN rules. The modeling approach is beyond the scope of this book.

When we design a controller, we need to determine variables for input and output. The output variables represent the amount of operation by the controller, and thus they are determined by the control target. On the other hand, the decision of input variables depends on the particular situation. If, for example, human operators are observing some variables to determine the manual control strategy, we should investigate how the operators are acting.

Generally, in multiple-input/multiple-output (MIMO) systems, it is difficult to generate control rules. Successful fuzzy logic control applications have mainly dealt with single-input/single-output (SISO) systems. It is hoped that fuzzy logic control can be applied to MIMO systems in the future. This chapter describes the design approach of fuzzy controllers for SISO systems.

5.2 Designing Fuzzy Logic Controllers

In this section, I describe the design procedure of fuzzy logic controllers for SISO target systems.

The designing of a fuzzy logic controller involves the construction of control rules. In many cases, we can obtain control rules by writing down the operators' actions in the IF-THEN format. Therefore there is no generic method of constructing control rules.

In addition, we may construct IF-THEN rules not only from operators' actions but from the response characteristic of the target system. In such cases, fuzzy logic controllers have been designed according to the procedure shown in Figure 5.1.

The design procedure includes the following steps:

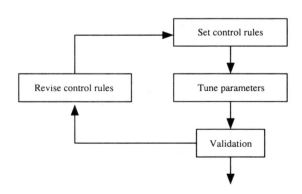

FIGURE 5.1. Design procedure of fuzzy controller.

1. construction of the control rules;
2. parameter tuning (to determine the fuzzy sets); and
3. validation and revision of control rules.

I have mentioned that we need to determine control rules for the design of fuzzy logic controllers. However, determining the control rules is not straightforward because the procedure includes the identification of parameters for fuzzy sets. We can assume that the parameters of fuzzy sets represent the parameters for the fuzzy logic controller. Therefore parameter tuning means to tune the parameters for the fuzzy sets included in the control rules. It is possible to improve the performance of the controller by such parameter tuning. However, parameter tuning alone sometimes cannot improve the controller's performance. This is because of inadequate construction of control rules. In this case, we can improve the performance by revising the control rules and tuning the parameters for the new rules.

I next describe the construction of control rules, and then parameter tuning methods. Finally, the revision of control rules is discussed.

5.2.1 Construction of Control Rules

The construction of control rules starts with determining what to select for input variables. Output variables are implicitly determined by operating targets. For input variables, a deviation from a set point, its variation (derivative), and its accumulation (integral) are often used. Conventional linear PI (Proportional-Integral), PD (Proportional-Derivative), and PID (Proportional-Integral-Derivative) controllers employ such input variables. For example, a PD-controller is described by the equation:

$$u = k_p(e + T_p\dot{e}).$$

Also, a PI-controller is described by

$$\dot{u} = k_p\left(\dot{e} + \frac{1}{T_1}e\right).$$

In the preceding equations, e denotes the deviation from a set point. If the output is u, we call the controller a position-type. If the output is $\dot{u}$, we call the controller a speed-type. k_p, T_1, and T_p are called proportional gain, integral time, and derivative time, respectively. Those are the parameters of the controller.

In fuzzy logic control, if a controller yields u from e and $\dot{e}$, we call it a fuzzy PD-controller. Similarly, if it yields only $\dot{u}$, we call it a fuzzy PI-controller. The respective controllers' rules can be described as follows.

- Fuzzy PI-controller:

  IF e is A and $\dot{e}$ is B THEN $\dot{u}$ is C (5.1)

- Fuzzy PD-controller:

  IF e is A and $\dot{e}$ is B THEN u is C (5.2)

TABLE 5.2.1.   Control rule tables for fuzzy PI-controller.

Rule Table (1)

		$\dot{e}$						
		NB	NM	NS	Z	PS	PM	PB
e	NB				NB			
	NM				NM			
	NS				NS			
	Z	NB	NM	NS	Z	PS	PM	PB
	PS				PS			
	PM				PM			
	PB				PB			

Rule Table (2)

		$\dot{e}$						
		NB	NM	NS	Z	PS	PM	PB
e	NB				NB	NM		
	NM				NM			
	NS				NS	ZO		PM
	Z	NB	NM	NS	Z	PS	PM	PB
	PS	NM		ZO	PS			
	PM				PM			
	PB			PM	PB			

We focus on PI-controllers in the rest of this section.

Because the fuzzy PI-controller has two variables in the premise part, we can summarize the control rules into a control rule table such as Table 5.2.1. It is common to apply the fuzzy sets for e and $\dot{e}$, composed of three positive and three negative with zero, as shown in Figure 5.2. The label means:

PB = Positive Big

PM = Positive Medium

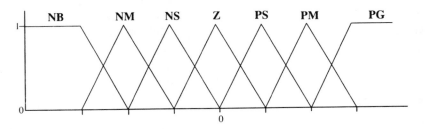

FIGURE 5.2. Fuzzy sets for fuzzy PI-controllers.

PS = Positive Small

Z   = zero

NS = Negative Small

NM = Negative Medium

NB = Negative Big

The rule table in Table 5.2.1 can then be read, for example, as

IF e is PB and $\dot{e}$ is Z THEN $\dot{u}$ is PB

The blank in the table does not trigger any rule, resulting in no inference. That is, at the blank points $\dot{u} = 0$, which means u is constant. PD-controllers, however, take position-type output u and the blank spots can cause trouble. This is because in the blank spots the output becomes zero ($u = 0$) resulting in no operation.

The difference between the preceding Rule tables (1) and (2) is the number of rules. Obviously, the greater the number of rules, the better chance we have for achieving the control target. However, if the control performance is the same, it is better to have a small number of rules. This is because the fewer rules we have, the simpler the parameter tuning, described in Section 5.2.2, becomes.

We can construct a rule table like Table 5.2.1 by considering response characteristics. Figure 5.3 shows the relationship between the rule table and response characteristics. Figure 5.3(a) shows a general time response and (b) depicts the behavior of the response on a phase (e–$\dot{e}$) plane. Figure 5.3(c) is the rotated figure of the rule table given in Table 5.2.1(1) so that the axis will correspond with those of the phase-plane response of (b). By comparing (b) and (c), we can grasp the relationship between the response and the rules. For example, starting from $e > 0$, $\dot{e}$ should be positive until e exceeds a set point, and then it switches to the negative $\dot{u}$. The set point is given at the origin of the phase plane. Also, as the distance from the origin (the set point) increases, a larger absolute value of control should be taken.

Next, let us look at Table 5.2.1 (2). There are six more rules than (1). In the additional rules,

IF e is PB and $\dot{e}$ is NS THEN $\dot{u}$ is PM

and

IF e is NB and $\dot{e}$ is PS THEN $\dot{u}$ is NM

improves the initial response. In Table 5.2.1(1), if e = PB and $\dot{e}$ = Z, $\dot{u}$ = PB and $\dot{u}$ is then maintained at zero until e changes its sign. However, due to the additional rule in Table 5.2.1(2), if e = PB and $\dot{e}$ = NS, there is additional control of $\dot{u}$ = PM, which improves the initial response.

On the other hand, in the additional six rules of Table 5.2.1(2),

IF e is PS and $\dot{e}$ is NB THEN $\dot{u}$ is NM

and

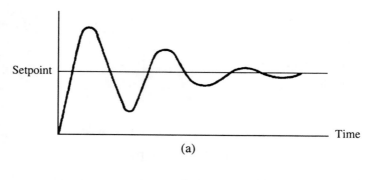

(a)

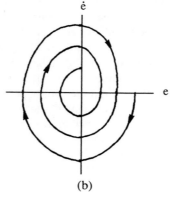

(b)

		NB	NM	NS	e Z	PS	PM	PB
	PB				PB			
	PM				PM			
	PS				PS			
$\dot{e}$	Z	NB	NM	NS	Z	PS	PM	PB
	NS				NS			
	NM				NM			
	NB				NB			

(c)

FIGURE 5.3. Response characteristic: (a) time, (b) phase, and control rule table (c).

IF e is NS and $\dot{e}$ is PB THEN $\dot{u}$ is PM

dampen the overshoot. In Table 5.2.1(1), if e = PB and $\dot{e}$ = Z, $\dot{u}$ = PB, there will be no negative operation until e exceeds the set point. However, by Rule (2), negative operation is taken shortly before e exceeds the set point, and this operation can dampen the overshoot.

If we thus determine the control rule table, the remaining design procedure is to determine the fuzzy sets. The parameters defining the fuzzy sets NB–PB also define the control parameters in a fuzzy logic controller. The following discussion focuses on parameter tuning.

5.2.2 Parameter Tuning

Once the control rules are determined, as in Table 5.2.1, the next step is to tune the parameters involved. The parameters here refer to the parameters of membership functions that define the fuzzy sets. Parameter tuning thus affects the shape of fuzzy sets. For fuzzy logic control, triangular and exponential fuzzy sets are often used. This section deals with the tuning of triangular fuzzy sets, which are most popular.

The tuning method can be roughly divided into these types:

type-1:   three parameters of each fuzzy set are to be tuned;

type-2:   one parameter of each fuzzy set is to be tuned; and

type-3:   the scaling factor of the total set is to be tuned.

Obviously, type-2 is simpler than type-1 and type-3 is simpler than type-2. Figure 5.4 shows the three types of parameter tuning.

Triangular fuzzy sets can be generally described by three parameters. By varying these three parameters, we can change the shape of the fuzzy sets in detail. This is the type-1 method. For the fuzzy sets shown in Figure 5.4 (a) the parameters to be tuned are 18 (P_1–P_{18}) in total.

If we find the tuning of all these parameters cumbersome, we can alternatively apply the type-2 method. In this method, there is a constraint of

$$\mu_A(x) + \mu_B(x) = 1 \quad \text{for all } x$$

on the adjacent fuzzy sets A and B. Therefore the fuzzy sets can be tuned by the parameter defining their peak ($= 1$) values. As a result, the number of parameters to be tuned declines to six (P_1–P_6).

Type-3 further reduces the number of parameters. This type assumes that the bases of the triangular fuzzy sets are all the same, in addition to the constraint of type-2. Therefore the only one parameter is to be tuned. Because this parameter determines the scaling of fuzzy sets, it is called the scaling factor. The fewer the parameters to be tuned, the simpler the tuning. The type-3 method is quite effective when there are a large number of variables to be tuned.

How much of the control performance is improved by the tuning of the parameter in the type-3 method is shown as follows.

Let us suppose the control target is represented by a first-order system such as

$$\frac{K}{Ts + 1}.$$

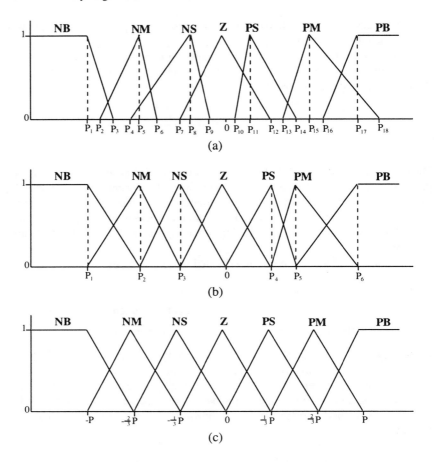

FIGURE 5.4. Parameter tuning of fuzzy sets: (a) type-1; (b) type-2; (c) type-3.

The control result as $T = 30$ and $K = 3$ is shown in Figure 5.5. Control rules of Table 5.2.1(1) are applied. S_e is the scaling factor for the error e (deviation from the set point). S_{de} is the scaling factor for $\dot{e}$ and S_{du} is the scaling factor of $\dot{u}$. In Figure 5.5, response is measured for three different values of S_{de}. As seen from this figure, the adequate selection of the scaling factor contributes to the improvement of control results.

By reducing the value of the scaling factor, even if the value of e and $\dot{e}$ are the same, we can apply control rules that are far apart from the origin of the e-$\dot{e}$ plane. This means we can regulate the gain of the fuzzy logic controller to some extent by the scaling factor.

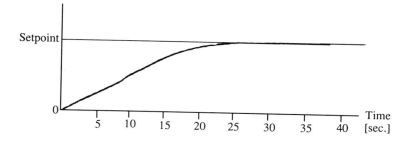

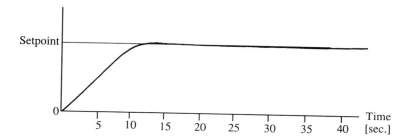

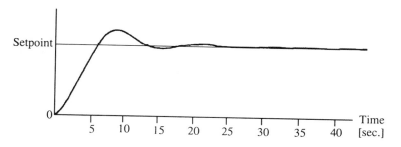

FIGURE 5.5. Control response by the rules of Table 5.2.1(1): (a) $S_e = 15$, $S_{de} = 3$, and $S_{du} = 50$; (b) $S_e = 15$, $S_{de} = 6$, and $S_{du} = 50$; (c) $S_e = 15$, $S_{de} = 12$, and $S_{du} = 50$.

5.2.3 Revision of Control Rules

Although I have mentioned the possibility of improving control performance by parameter tuning, the effect of parameter tuning can be almost null if the construction of the control rules is wrong. If such is the case, we can improve the situation by (a) adding necessary rules; and (b) deleting rules that are adversely affecting the control performance.

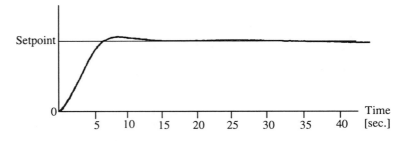

FIGURE 5.6. Control response by the rules of Table 5.2.1 (2).

For the results of Figure 5.5, I have already shown the control performance of the rules given in Table 5.2.1(1). The result of the extended rules listed in Table 5.2.1(2) is now given in Figure 5.6. Here, $S_e = 15$, $S_{de} = 6$, and $S_{du} = 50$.

The addition of rules may be an attempt to improve control performance but if an excess number of rules is added, the improvement is sluggish and the resultant system is less visible to the designer.

It is relatively easy to locate a rule that adversely affects the control results because we can investigate which rule is employed to produce the present control output. When the idle time of control is relatively short, in particular, we can improve the control performance by revising or deleting the rule that is used to produce the adverse effect in the control result.

5.3 Application Examples of Fuzzy Reasoning

In this section, I show the readers the following two examples: control of a steam engine, and combination control of fuzzy logic and PID control.

5.3.1 Control of a Steam Engine

Fuzzy logic control was first proposed by Mamdani in 1974. The target of the fuzzy logic control was a model steam engine. Figure 5.7 shows the control system of the steam engine.

The goal of the control is to regulate the outlet pressure and the engine speed so both are constant. The operation input is the supplied heat to the boiler and the throttle opening of the engine. Figure 5.8 shows the control rules. The rules are grouped for each operation input. Fuzzy sets in the rules are given in a discrete form as shown in Table 5.3.1. Figure 5.9 shows the control result.

Because this steam engine has a nonlinear characteristic, the PID-controller did not produce good results. Also, over a certain period, parameters have to be tuned because the system changes over time. Fuzzy logic controllers do not need such frequent tuning of parameters and reportedly produced better results.

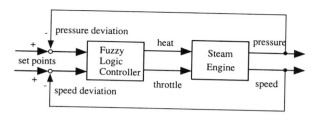

FIGURE 5.7. Fuzzy control system of steam engine.

5.3.2 *Combination Control of PID and Fuzzy Control*

It is common to apply fuzzy logic control by itself, but I introduce here an example of combination control with a conventional controller for improved effect in attaining control goals. This example is a control system to regulate the constant outlet temperature of a furnace in a hydrogen production plant.

Before the application of fuzzy logic, PID control was used. However, because the idle time of the system is large, PID control alone was not sufficient to attain the goal and thus it needed the intervention of operators. In this application, fuzzy logic replaces the operators' intervention and aims at full automation. The outline of the hydrogen production plant is shown in Figure 5.10.

HEATER ALGORITHM

       If PE = NB then if CPE = not (NB or NM) then HC = PB

or

       If PE = NB or NM then if CPE = NS then HC = PM

or

       If PE = NS then if CPE = PS or NO then HC = PM

or

       If PE = NO then if CPE = PB or PM then HC = PM

THROTTLE ALGORITHM

       If SE = PO then if CSE = PB then TC = NS

or

       If SE = PS then if CSE = PB or PM then TC = NS

or

       If SE = PM then if CSE = PB or PM or PS then TC = NS

or

       If SE = PB then if CSE = not (NB or NM) then TC = NB

       PB = Positive Big, PM = Positive Medium,
       PS = Positive Small, PO = Positive Zero, N = Negative

FIGURE 5.8. Control rules for steam engine control.

TABLE 5.3.1.   Discrete fuzzy sets for steam engine control.

(a) Premise-part variables (PE, SE)

	$-P_6$	$-P_5$	$-P_4$	$-P_3$	$-P_2$	$-P_1$	$-P_0$	P_0	P_1	P_2	P_3	P_4	P_5	P_6
PB	0	0	0	0	0	0	0	0	0	0	0.1	0.4	0.8	1.0
PM	0	0	0	0	0	0	0	0	0	0.2	0.7	1.0	0.7	0.2
PS	0	0	0	0	0	0	0	0.3	0.8	1.0	0.5	0.1	0	0
P0	0	0	0	0	0	0	0	1.0	0.6	0.1	0	0	0	0
N0	0	0	0	0	0.1	0.6	1.0	0	0	0	0	0	0	0
NS	0	0	0.1	0.5	1.0	0.8	0.3	0.	0	0	0	0	0	0
NM	0.2	0.7	1.0	0.7	0.2	0	0	0	0	0	0			
NB	1.0	0.8	0.4	0.1	0	0	0	0	0	0	0			

(b) Premise-part variables (CPE, CSE)

	$-P_6$	$-P_5$	$-P_4$	$-P_3$	$-P_2$	$-P_1$	P_0	P_1	P_2	P_3	P_4	P_5	P_6
PB	0	0	0	0	0	0	0	0	0	0.1	0.4	0.8	1.0
PM	0	0	0	0	0	0	0	0	0.2	0.7	1.0	0.7	0.2
PS	0	0	0	0	0	0	0	0.9	1.0	0.7	0.2	0	0
N0	0	0	0	0	0	0.5	1.0	0.5	0	0	0	0	0
NS	0	0	0.2	0.7	1.0	0.9	0	0	0	0	0	0	0
NM	0.2	0.7	1.0	0.7	0.2	0	0	0	0	0	0	0	0
NB	1.0	0.8	0.4	0.1	0	0	0	0	0	0	0	0	0

(c) Consequence-part variables (HC)

	$-P_7$	$-P_6$	$-P_5$	$-P_4$	$-P_3$	$-P_2$	$-P_1$	P_0	P_1	P_2	P_3	P_4	P_5	P_6	P_7
PB	0	0	0	0	0	0	0	0	0	0	0.1	0.1	0.4	0.8	1.0
PM	0	0	0	0	0	0	0	0	0	0.2	0.7	1.0	0.7	0.2	0
PS	0	0	0	0	0	0	0	0.4	1.0	0.8	0.4	0.1	0	0	0
N0	0	0	0	0	0	0	0.2	1.0	0.2	0	0	0	0	0	0
NS	0	0	0	0.1	0.4	0.8	1.0	0.4	0	0	0	0	0	0	0
NM	0	0.2	0.7	1.0	0.7	0.2	0	0	0	0	0	0	0	0	0
NB	1.0	0.8	0.4	0.1	0	0	0	0	0	0	0	0	0	0	0

(d) Consequence-part variables (TC)

	$-P_2$	$-P_1$	P_0	P_1	P_2
PB	0	0	0	0.5	1.0
PS	0	0	0.5	1.0	0.5
N0	0	0.5	1.0	0.5	0
NS	0.5	1.0	0.5	0	0
NB	1.0	0.5	0	0	0

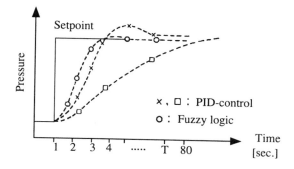

FIGURE 5.9. Control results of PID controller and fuzzy logic controller.

If the outlet temperature of the furnace is not maintained constant, it adversely affects the catalytic agent in the desulfurization tower in the next process. When the PID-controller alone was applied, there were such problems as:

a. This system regulated the hydrogen supply header and automatically regulated the amount of hydrogen production depending on the demand from other parts of the plant.
b. In the material heating furnace, materials were rapidly heated from normal temperature to more than 350°C. Therefore a slight variation in the amount of production changed the evaporation point drastically.
c. The fuel for the furnace was the off-gas from the plant and it changed its characteristic.
d. The switching of materials was frequent due to the plant's gas balance or other reasons.

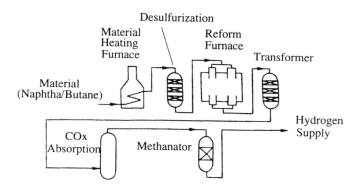

FIGURE 5.10. Outline of hydrogen production plant.

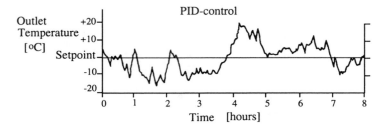

FIGURE 5.11. Control result of PID-controller.

Such factors as those listed made the control of outlet temperature very difficult. As shown in Figure 5.11, even in a normal operation, the outlet temperature constantly fluctuated as much as 15°C from the target value. A feedforward control was also attempted for this system, but it could not trace the material switching and thus needed a manual intervention. To solve these difficulties, a control system was developed to combine fuzzy logic and the PID-controller. The structure of the control system is given in Figure 5.12.

The combined system aims at periodically compensating the output of the PID-controller by fuzzy logic. There are a total of 17 rules representing the operators' know-how. Some of the fuzzy control rules are given in the following.

(a) IF   the outlet temperature is slightly higher than

             the target value

     AND   the variation of the outlet temperature is rather

             large on the positive side,

     THEN   close the control valve a little.

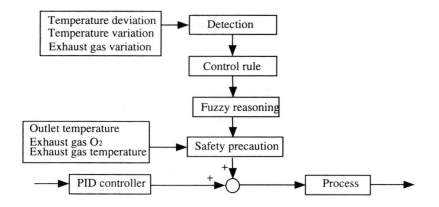

FIGURE 5.12. Structure of combined control system of fuzzy logic and PID-controller.

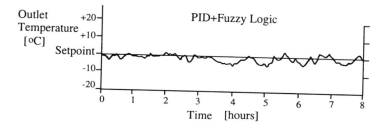

FIGURE 5.13. Control result of combination control.

(b) IF   the outlet temperature is much higher than
              the target value

     AND   the speed variation of exhaust gas temperature is
              rather large on the positive side,

     THEN   close the control valve a lot.

(c) IF   the outlet temperature is much higher than
              the target value

     AND   the speed variation of exhaust gas temperature is
              rather large on the negative side,

     THEN   maintain the control valve.

Figures 5.13 and 5.14 show the control results. From the results we conclude the
following:

i. In normal operating conditions, the outlet temperature was stabilized within
   the 5°C error of the target value.

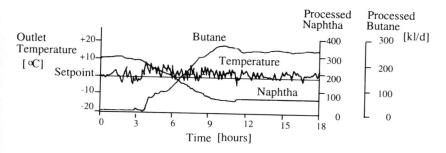

FIGURE 5.14. Control result when material is switched from naphtha to butane.

ii. Figure 5.14 shows the control result when the material was switched from naphtha to butane. This result shows automatic control is now possible even when the switching of the materials is involved.
iii. Startup and shutdown could be automated.

By the combination of fuzzy logic and the PID-controller, we have achieved the stabilization of normal operation, automatic control when switching materials, and during startup and shutdown. The reasons can be traced as follows.

a. The periodic compensation by fuzzy logic on PID control corresponds with the operators' action to supervise and regulate the system's behavior against the PID control.
b. Because the system is constantly supervised, there is no problem increasing the response rate of the PID-controller.

This type of combination control is effective in other control systems governed by conventional controllers with operator intervention.

References

[1] Sugeno, M. 1985. An introductory survey on fuzzy control. *Information Sciences*, 36: 59–83.
[2] Mamdani, E. H. 1974. Applications of fuzzy algorithms for control of a simple dynamic plant. *Proceedings of IEE* 121, 12: 1585–1588.

Index